Throwing Pots

THROWING POTS

Phil Rogers

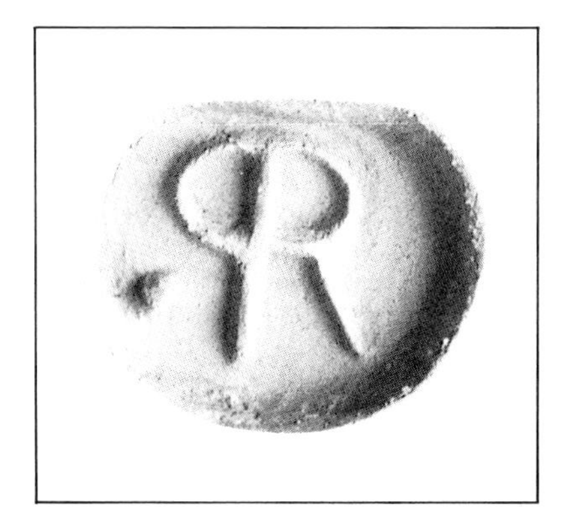

A & C Black • London

University of Pennsylvania Press • Philadelphia

A pot is a living thing. Its association so markedly human. We talk of the foot, the belly, the shoulder, the neck and the lip and we intuitively feel a good pot's honesty, strength, nobility or charm much as we do with people . . . Sometimes one can speak of a wet, newly thrown pot in which every movement is like frozen music. Life flowing for a few moments through the hands of a potter.

Bernard Leach

First published in Great Britain
A & C Black (Publishers) Limited
37 Soho Square
London W1D 3QZ

ISBN 0–7136–5723–5

Published simultaneously in the USA by
University of Pennsylvania Press
4200 Pine Street
Philadelphia, PA 19104-4011

Reprinted 2001

ISBN 0-8122-1757-8

A CIP catalogue record for this book is available from the British Library and the US Library of Congress.

Filmset in 10/12 Photina by August Filmsetting, Haydock
Printed in Hong Kong by Wing King Tong Co., Ltd

Cover illustrations
front: Jar by the Author
back: Pitcher by the Author

Frontispiece
Two salt-glazed pitchers by the Author.
The taller example is 15 in/38 cm tall and thrown from 12 lb/5.5 kg of clay.

Title page
The author's potter's mark. All potters, even aspiring ones, should make their own seal mark and then use it with discrimination.

Contents

Acknowledgements

I would like to thank Peter Harper for his care and patience in producing the clear and informative black and white sequence photographs. Thanks to Potterycrafts who supplied the potter's wheel that we used in the photographs. My sincere thanks also to all the potters who kindly supplied photographs of their work: Nigel Lambert, Sarah Walton, Jeff Oestrich, Joseph Bennion, Peter Beard, Josie Walter, Jim Malone, Svend Bayer, Ruthanne Tudball, Micki Schloessingk, Sandra Lockwood, Mark Hewitt, Nic Collins, Duncan Ross and David Frith. Thanks also to the Crafts Study Centre in Bath for the photograph of the Korean honey pot.

My appreciation for her faith in me to produce this book to Linda Lambert at A & C Black.

British potters are well-known around the world for their openness and willingness to share hard won knowledge and information. My thanks go to all those well-established potters who were kind enough to help me when I was starting out. Amongst others, Michael Casson, John Maltby, David Frith, John Leach, Pete Starkey and the late Nick Edison-Giles.

Introduction

For many years I have organised and taught pottery summer schools here at my pottery in Wales. Over the years the workshop has played host to potters of various abilities from all over the world, every one eager to either learn how to throw pots or to improve their already developing throwing skills.

During this time I have developed a teaching method which seems to meet with some enthusiasm. It is based upon a direct and easy to follow progression through the various skills that are required to make good pottery. I endeavour to make the learning of skills as much fun as possible and to take away the drudgery of repetitive practice that so often dulls the most enthusiastic of appetites. Through the pages of this book I shall try to recapture the learning atmosphere of one of our summer workshops in the hope that it will inspire as it instructs.

Trying to learn to throw pots from a book is a little like reading the ABC of Brain Surgery or Build your own Space

The house and pottery set amongst the beautiful countryside of Mid-Wales.

Shuttle in ten weekly parts. It's not easy! No book can totally replace hands-on-tuition with a thoroughly competent and hopefully, inspiring potter-teacher. There are basic skills that have to be learnt, often by dogged practice, before a confidence evolves that allows the potter to make pots unfettered by the restraints of inadequate skill. Although, paradoxically, it is often the case that the relatively unskilled or 'naive' student can produce work that is fresh and lively simply because too much 'greater' skill hasn't got in the way of a direct approach to the clay. Shoji Hamada, the famous Japanese potter, once said that he felt that he had become *too* good a thrower. By this he meant that his skill restricted him in that he could not allow himself to be as expressive with the clay as he would like. His solution to this dilemma was to revolve his wheel in the opposite direction!

My hope is that the reader will use this book in conjunction with a sustained period of tuition possibly at an evening class or local education college or, more suitably, a week or more intensive learning at the workshop of a practising potter.

A residential course, where you are free to learn for a sustained period without the day to day concerns and worries of every day life, is by far the best way of making real progress. Evening classes can be perfectly good but a lot depends upon the teacher's ability and commitment. Often, there are too many people wanting to use too little equipment and your precious work sits on its allotted shelf during the intervening week at the mercy of whoever uses that studio before your next visit.

There are more and more residential courses appearing each year. Most are run by accomplished potters at their own studios, often providing on-site accommodation and meals. Sadly though, not all are exactly what we would expect them to be and it is worthwhile doing some research before booking to attend any summer workshop. Nearly all of the worthwhile courses are advertised in *Ceramic Review* or, for American readers, *Ceramics Monthly* but before you book to attend one of them I suggest you:

Dinner plate by Mark Hewitt (USA), 11 in/ 28 cm. This seemingly simple plate displays the attention to finish and correctness of proportion one would expect from a professional potter. Mark Hewitt works in North Carolina and is deeply influenced by the making traditions and materials available in that part of the USA. This plate is decorated with gestural marks through an iron based slip under an Albany slip glaze. The stained glass has melted into the surface to create a stark landscape.

a. Check that you actually like the work of the tutor involved and that his or her work is of good quality. Send away for the course details and take up any references that might be offered.
b. Try to talk to someone who has already attended that particular course. It is very important to get a

personal recommendation.

c. Visit the workshop beforehand if that's possible.
d. Make some enquiries about the standards of accommodation and the meals etc. that are provided.

The world, it seems, was designed for potters. We can find all that we need to make perfectly functional, beautiful pottery from our immediate surroundings: clay to form the body of our pots and, sometimes, the slips and glazes to cover them. Rocks and the ashes from plants and trees can provide us with glazes. Pure salt can miraculously form a glaze when introduced into the mysterious alchemy of a searingly hot kiln.

It is this very elemental nature of the craft coupled with a long and revered history that attracts people to it. Throwing clay on a potter's wheel and the seemingly effortless and wonderful way that the clay will swell and climb in the hands of a skilled potter is merely the beginning to this most 'natural' and ancient of crafts.

The potter is called upon to be many things other than a thrower or former of pots. Labourer, electrician, bricklayer, carpenter, chemist, artist and pyrotechnician are just some of the hats that have to be worn. But, for now, we shall concentrate on throwing and leave all those other facets to other books from this same series.

Hopefully this book with its clear and informative photographs by Peter Harper will illuminate and clarify some of those tricky areas that you may have had problems with. Remember though, it is not enough to merely learn the mechanics of throwing. To be able to throw clay upwards and outwards is of little use without some judgement as to what constitutes a good form or a bad form. For this reason I shall be attempting, with the help of some photographs of exemplary pots, to offer some guidance as to the questions that you will need to ask yourself about the pots that you make.

Chapter One
Equipment

Potter's wheel

In his book *The World of Japanese Ceramics*, Herbert Sanders tells us that the earliest potter's wheel of the Orient was a circular pad of woven matting that the potter turned by hand. I have seen such 'wheels' in use today in East Africa. Ethiopian women make the traditional cooking and drinking pots by this very method, skilfully turning the mat with one hand whilst at the same time pinching and coaxing the clay with the other.

The potter's wheel as we understand it today in the West first saw the light of day in the Middle East some 5,000 years BC and has come a long way since its earliest beginnings as a flat disc of wood suspended on a crude wooden bearing. In many parts of the world these early wheels are still being used to make fine pots. Hamada, at his workshop in Mashiko, used a wheel which was revolved by means of a stick that was inserted into the wheel's surface and spun much in the manner of a child's spinning top. It is the weight of the wheel that provided the momentum for its movement. In modern, non-motorised wheels the weight has been transferred to a fly wheel underneath the turntable which is turned by a simple treadle or geared pedal.

For all the advances that have been made in the construction and efficiency of the modern potter's wheel, some would argue that technical progress has been at the expense of certain qualities in the finished pot that can only be obtained having been made on a wheel where potter and wheel are in close harmony. There is much scope for the potter with woodworking and simple engineering skills to make his own potter's wheel and a number of plans have been published to enable you to do this. Personally, I feel that excellent pots can be made on any type of wheel, as ultimately it is the potter and his 'feeling' for the clay that really counts.

Traditional Ethiopian cooking pot, d. 11 in. Made from a coarse local clay, this pot has a rounded bottom that allows it to be set upon an open flame without cracking. It is made by the left hand pinching and forming the clay while the right hand revolves the rush mat on which the clay sits. The outer surface has been coated with a mixture of oil and ochre and then polished before being fired in a pit with Eucalyptus leaves and twigs.

The Japanese potter Shoji Hamada sitting at his wheel. The large wooden turntable is set in a pit surrounded by a wooden stage on which the potter sits. Most Western potters would find the level of this wheel in relation to the body extremely uncomfortable. The wheel is revolved by means of a stick which locates in a hole at the wheel's outer edge. Effectively the wheel is always slowing down which means that the potter works in 'tune' with his wheel. This characteristic rhythmic action of the wheel had a profound effect upon Hamada's pots.

A compact and portable potter's wheel built in New Zealand and supplied in the UK by Potterycrafts Ltd. At the lower end of the price range. I would recommend this type of wheel for the enthusiastic beginner or hobby potter. Its size means that it can be stowed away when not in use yet it is strong enough to handle large weights of clay.

In the West though, by far the majority of potter's wheels are now turned by electricity, often with quite sophisticated electronic variable speeds or sometimes with what is known as a cone drive. Either is fine. In fact, the potter has a daunting choice in the number of wheels available and after considerations of the pocket, I would say that comfort in the working position is probably the most important factor to influence your choice, especially if you have any intention at all of spending rather a lot of time making pots. It is worth noting that backache is often referred to as 'The Potter's Disease' and the throwing position is definitely a contributory factor. When choosing your wheel these are a few points to bear in mind:

1. *Try your chosen wheel before you buy it*

Having chosen the wheel you think might be right for you, endeavour to find someone who has the same wheel and try throwing a few pots with it. Feel for the comfort or discomfort. Are you severely hunched over? Is it difficult to operate the speed control whilst at the same time being able to bend for a view of the pot? If the answer to either of these questions is yes, then this wheel may be too small for you. Your comfort while throwing is very important. It is almost impossible to find a seated position at a potter's wheel that is perfectly comfortable but you must try, right from the very beginning, to sit with your back as straight as possible. Avoid prolonged, extreme bending in order to see the profile of a form. I know from personal experience that your back will suffer for it later on.

2. *Make sure you have an adequate sized slop tray*

It is very annoying to constantly have to stop work to empty an undersized slop tray.

3. *Buy with confidence*

If you are buying your wheel new rather than 'secondhand', give consideration to the company that you are buying it from. There will inevitably come the time that you will require spares or repairs and it's nice to think that the company will still be around when you need them. Most of the pottery wheels supplied by the potters' merchants have a good spares back up available. Indeed many of the component parts are standard engineering stock and available from engineering factors.

4. *Buy the best that you can afford*

As I have said, there is a huge choice available on the market. Buy the best quality wheel that you can afford bearing in mind the job that it will have to do. For instance, there would be little point in buying the wheel illustrated if you were embarking upon a career in large flowerpot making. Conversely, an expensive 'professional' wheel may be unnecessary if you are intending pottery as a part-time hobby activity.

5. *Secondhand?*

There is a lively secondhand market for ceramic equipment and it is well worth checking the classified ads in magazines such as *Ceramic Review* or *Ceramics Monthly*. People often purchase equipment and then find that pottery wasn't for them after all. Bargains can be found, often at a fraction of the new cost but be sure to check that the manufacturer still exists if you are not the engineering 'do it yourself' type.

Tools

Having found your wheel or secured the use of one, you will need some basic tools to start you off. A potter's tool box very quickly becomes a kind of personal treasure chest that to the non-potter would seem an unlikely assortment of junk! Many of your tools can be simply and quickly made at home. Others may be purchased from a potters' supply company but may also be found for much less cost at the local DIY store or kitchen shop. I have found that the best time to buy tools from the potters' supply companies is at one of the potters'

A selection of my own tools. Some I have made myself, some I have had made for me and others I have bought. The pots that you make are, in some ways, a reflection of the tools that you use. It is also true that a new tool can be the catalyst for new ideas.

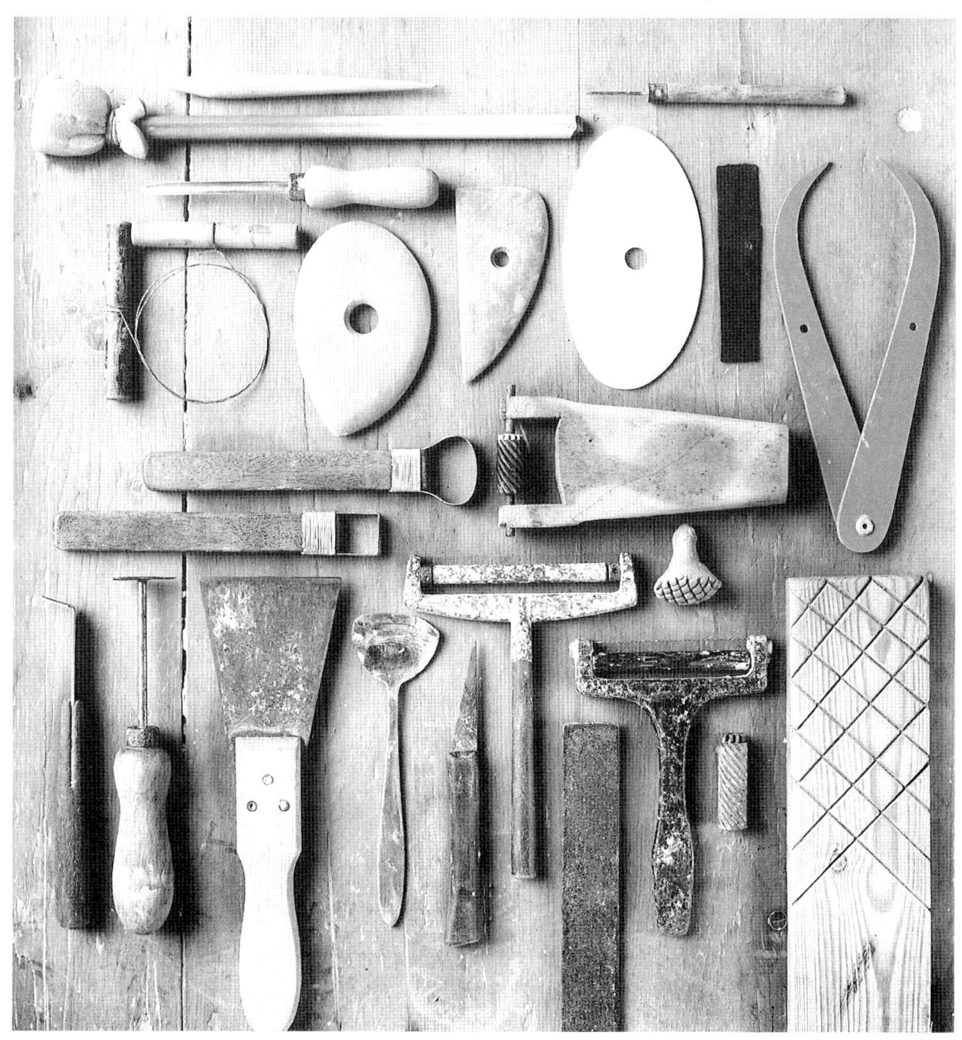

festivals that are popular at the moment where tools are often discounted to clear stock.

Of the tools illustrated on page 14, initially, as a 'starter set', you will require the following:

1. A selection of ribs

The potter's rib, so called because that's exactly what it used to be, a cow's rib, is useful for shaping the outside of your pots and removing water or slip. It also strengthens the pot by consolidating the clay. Ribs can be easily made from perspex off-cuts especially if you have a bench grinding wheel.

2. A needle

Every potter occasionally finds an air bubble in the clay and the needle can be used to prick it. At the beginning you will find that a needle is useful for trimming the top rim of a pot that has become uneven. As your skills increase, you will find that you need to do this less and less often.

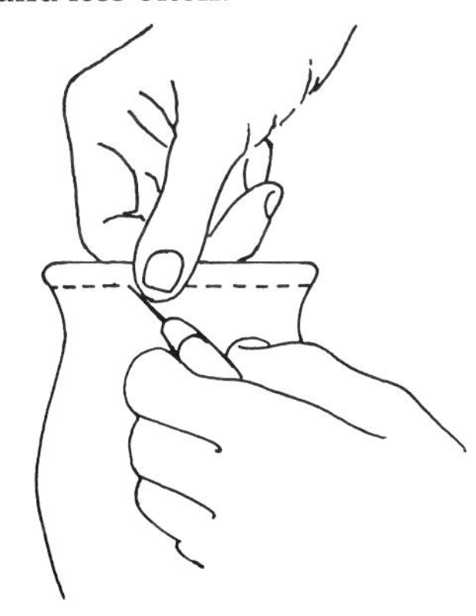

Using a needle to cut off an unwanted or uneven rim.

Let the clay revolve through the thumb and forefinger. Rest the needle on the end of your thumb. With the needle angled back and the wheel on a slow speed gently push the point through the pot until it appears on the other side. Calmly lift the rim away with thumb and forefinger.

3. A sponge on a stick

(approx. 9 in./23 cm)

Useful for taking the water from the inside of a thrown form when it is either too tall or too narrow for the fingers. Can also be used as a throwing stick. See page 33.

4. A turning tool

I prefer the 'looped' type which, to me at least, seems to cut through the clay more cleanly than the solid blade.

5. A small piece of soft leather. Not chamois leather. (See page 33.)

It is used for rounding, smoothing and consolidating the rims of your pots.

6. A twisted wire secured at each end with a toggle

I use modelmaker's wire available from modelmakers' supplies shops. An alternative is trace wire used in angling which has the benefit of being stainless steel. Make yourself two wires, one from lightweight wire for cutting off your pots and another from heavyweight wire for wedging.

7. A flat metal strip with chisel ends

(This one is an engineering hacksaw with the teeth ground away.)

Useful for all sorts of throwing techniques: lids, rims, ridges and decorative lines etc.

8. A bench scraper which doubles as a bat scraper also

9. A turning tool that has a point in the shape of its head. (See page 33.)

I use this type of cutting tool for placing a bevel or chamfer at the base of my pots.

10. A small piece of soft upholsterer's foam

I do not like the natural sponge for throwing with because it has a granular texture which often leaves lines in the soft clay.

You will add other tools to your collection as and when the need arises or when you have a decorative idea that requires a particular tool. For instance, in the picture you will see a roller set in a wooden handle and a simple clay stamp. The roller is made from part of the internal workings of a pencil sharpener and the stamp is just clay that has been impressed with the handle end of a paintbrush. This type of tool is quickly and simply made and will help you to produce pots that are individual to you.

Try not to fall into the trap of believing that you have to have large numbers of shop bought tools. It's you that makes the pots, the tools only help. Lots of clever tools don't necessarily mean good pots.

Other sundry equipment

Throwing bats

I make all my pots on a 'bat' rather than directly on the metal wheel head. A bat is a circular piece of material, usually marine ply or chipboard that is positioned and secured on top of the metal wheel head, either by means of locating studs in the wheelhead and holes in the bat or simply by sticking it to a pad of soft clay. The benefits of using bats are that: a) pots that are either very wide or even flat can be lifted from the wheel still attached to the bat without distortion; b) pots that require further attention can easily be recentred on the wheel, and c) I simply prefer the feel of wood rather than cold metal under my hands.

I make my own bats quickly and cheaply from top grade chipboard by the use of a small jigsaw. I cut them in a variety of diameters to allow for the making of wide, shallow dishes and plates.

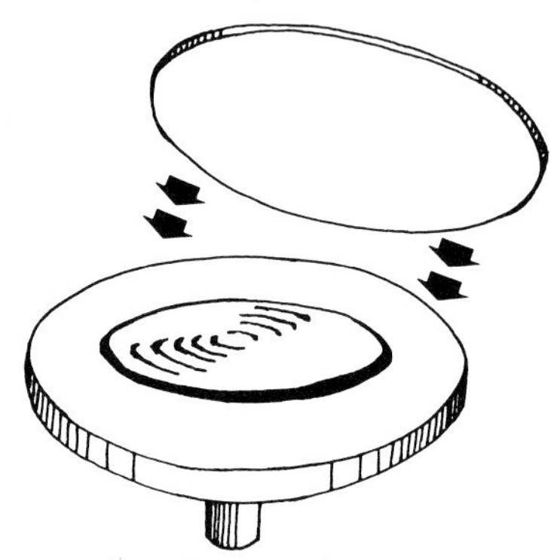

Throw a thin, flat disc of clay onto the wheelhead and then scribe a series of concentric grooves with a tool. Slightly dampen the back of the bat, place it in position and thump it down.

Other items

You will need a workbench or table set close to your wheel. From here you can take your prepared clay balls as you need them. You will also require some wareboards to take your pots as you make them. A wareboard is nothing more than a plywood shelf that can be placed onto wall brackets or a shelving rack within arms' reach as you sit at your wheel. This shelf can be replaced with another when you have filled it with pots and removed it to the drying rack.

A towel near to you is a good idea. You will frequently need to dry your hands, for instance, as you lift your smaller pots from the wheel, and you will also need a bowl to hold your water. Lastly, you will need an overall or apron. Whatever you choose, buy it in nylon rather than in cotton. Cotton holds onto dust and can quickly become a health hazard. Nylon is much less prone to do this and is more easily wiped clean.

Chapter Two
Clay

Clay is truly a miracle of nature and in common with most other miracles of nature we rather tend to take it for granted. Throughout time it has sheltered us, stored our food, allowed us to eat and to drink comfortably and with hygiene. It has brought us our water and carried away our effluents. It has been formed into some of the most beautiful and valuable artifacts that humanity has known. Indeed, it could be argued that the discovery of clay and its amazing properties formed the basis of man's civilisation in that man the hunter was transformed into man the farmer and settler as soon as he was able to store

Teabowl by Sandra Lockwood (Australia), 5 in/ 12.5 cm diam. The deliberate use of wet clay and a throwing technique that coaxes rather than bullies the clay has resulted in a bowl of great softness. The wood and salt-glaze fire has enhanced those organic qualities by creating a sumptuous, almost alabaster-like surface. *Photo by J Lascelles.*

the fruits of his labours for later consumption.

In nature, clays can vary enormously. Physically and chemically clays can be very different as can their colour, both when found and when they have been fired. Some clays are white and fire white, some are blue/grey and fire red, some are brown or black and fire red and others are grey and fire to a buff colour. Confused? Don't be. There are essentially two ways of obtaining the clay that you will need to throw your pots. You can either buy it ready to use or obtain the raw materials to enable you to prepare a clay 'body' for yourself.

A clay body

A 'clay body' is what we call a blend of clay and other minerals that the potter prepares to suit his own particular needs. Clay ***can*** be used 'as dug'. In the past, potteries appeared in particular locations simply because the raw materials that the potters required just happened to be there. Stoke-on-Trent became the main centre for pottery making in the United Kingdom because of an ample supply of good red clay and the seams of Staffordshire coal that fueled the kilns. Today, potters will often blend two or more different clays together or add sand or fireclay grog to their bodies. Sometimes these additions will improve the working properties of the clay and sometimes additions are made to alter its fired appearance. Both texture and fired colour can be adjusted in this way.

Before choosing the clay body most suitable, the potter has to make some fundamental decisions about the sort of pots that are to be made. Do you want to make earthenware, stoneware or maybe porcelain or raku? Each kind of pottery will have its own clay body and they can differ enormously. However, whatever or wherever your interests lie there will be a clay body particularly suited to you.

Clay for the wheel

The thrower requires his clay to have good plasticity together with the strength to withstand the stretching and bending of throwing and handle making. Plasticity is related to both the particle size of the body clay and the moisture content. Generally, plasticity improves as the particle size decreases and the moisture content increases. There are, of course, limits to the water content. Too much water and the clay becomes so soft that it is unusable; too little, and the clay is hard and unworkable. A good 'plastic' clay will stretch without rupturing, support itself during throwing and not 'slump' as the throwing nears its end. As a clay, it will also allow itself to be reshaped with a reasonably light pressure.

The plasticity of any clay can be improved by keeping. Clay is constructed of microscopic hexagonal crystals which are flat in section. The plasticity of clay relies on these crystals being able to slide one over the other when lubricated by water. During storage there is a build up of bacterial growth which creates a colloidal gel that lubricates the clay particles even further. When a clay has 'soured' as we call it, you will notice an odour a little like pond water and the clay becomes darker in colour. Well soured and smelly clay is prized and explains why potters often add mysterious agents to their mixture to aid this phenomenon. I often add vinegar or stale yoghurt to my clay mixes. It is said that the Chinese would add urine to achieve the same results but I draw the line just before this!

This is not really the book to delve too deeply into the chemistry of clay or indeed the business of creating your own 'body' recipe. However, if you decide that mixing your own body is not a practical proposition and buying your clay seems a more sensible approach then I would suggest the following.

Obtaining your clay

Write off to the potters' supplies companies whose names appear at the back of this book and ask them for samples of clays that seem, from their catalogue description, to suit your particular needs. Test these samples for 'throwability' and fired colour and choose ***just one*** to use. I would strongly recommend that you use only one clay at a time. It is very difficult to keep clays separate especially if you haven't a large workshop. Arbitrary and unrepeatable mixtures of different clays will cause problems in the future and create an inconsistency that is a serious barrier to progress.

Choosing the right clay body is extremely important. I know, from potters who have attended my own summer workshops, that there is a great deal of dissatisfaction with many of the proprietary, ready to use clays. I often find that people are amazed at the workability of my clay mix as compared to the clay that they are used to. They suddenly find that pots which were previously beyond their skill level are now perfectly possible. Plasticity in a clay body relies in large measure on the particle size of the constituent clays. Good quality, fine grained ball clays are not generally incorporated into the ready to use bodies in very high proportions. Firstly because they are comparatively expensive and secondly, because their fine grain size causes problems in the filter presses that are required to process such large quantities of clay.

I would say that, if it is at all possible, mixing your own clay body with a basis of fine ball clays is infinitely more preferable than buying the ready to use in its neat plastic bags. In this way, you will achieve exactly the clay that you want. Plasticity, texture, colour are all in your control as is the ability to change your 'mix' overnight if you wish to.

I realise, of course, that mixing one's own clay requires some equipment and space not least of all to store sacks of dry clay powder and that many beginners will not be able to entertain the idea. There are perfectly good clay bodies available, you just have to find the one that is most suited to the kind of pots that you want to make.

Clay preparation

However you choose to obtain your clay, you will need to prepare it for throwing probably immediately before you sit down at the wheel. It is essential that the thrower uses a clay that has been prepared properly. Poorly prepared clay, or clay that has been harshly treated after preparation, will make throwing very difficult indeed. Clay can come from the mixer or the plastic bag containing pockets of air that will show themselves as bubbles during throwing, frustrating even the skilled thrower. Your task in preparing the clay is to remove these bubbles and any inconsistency that may exist in the firmness of the clay.

Essentially there are two methods of achieving a homogenous, air-free clay: wedging and spiral kneading.

Wedging

By this method the clay is mixed and the air is eliminated by the controlled impact of clay upon clay. (a) Begin by taking as large a lump of clay as you can manage but it shouldn't be less than 10 lb/4.5 kg. Fashion the lump into a neat block on the wedging table and (b) slice it through the middle with a wire. (c) Take the top portion and lift it up above your head. (d) Now, with controlled force bring it down heavily upon the bottom portion. (e) The impact should burst any bubbles near to the surface. Pick up the whole block, turn it around, slice it through again and repeat the process. You will need to do this 20 or so times by which time your clay should be ready to spiral knead.

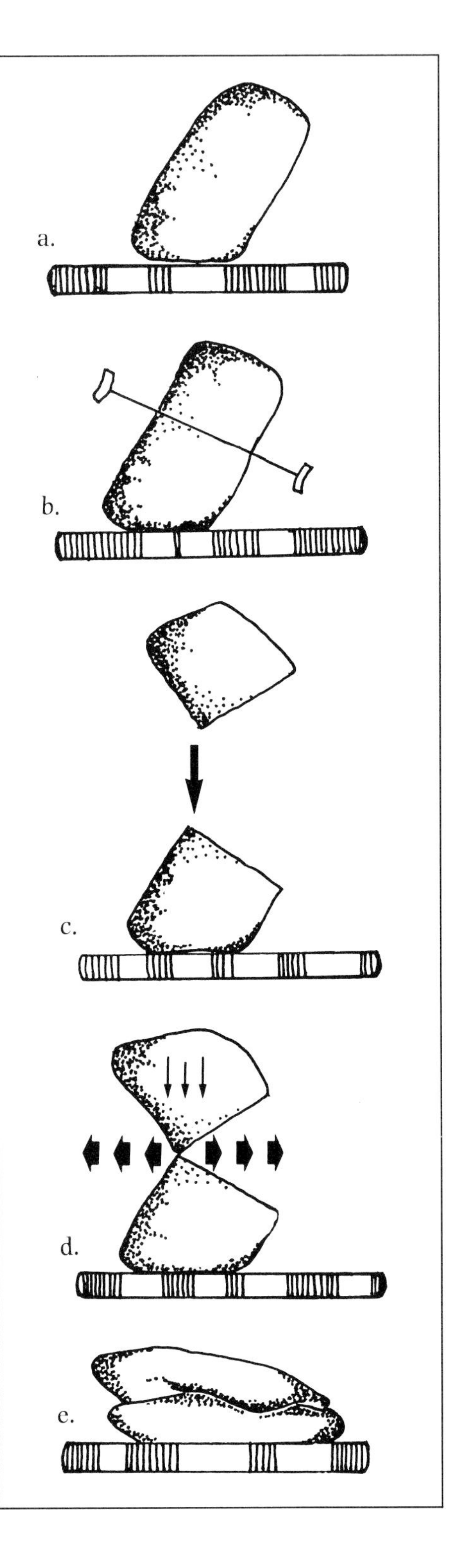

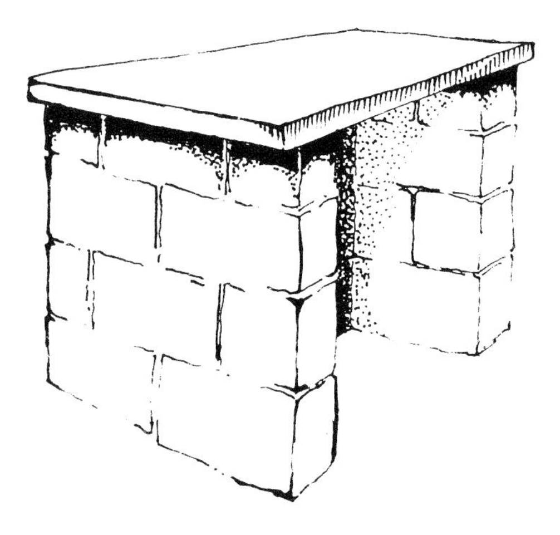

My wedging table is constructed from concrete blocks and a slab of Welsh slate although a concrete paving slab will do just as well. The construction needs to be sturdy as you will often be bashing heavy lumps of clay down onto it.

The height of your table should be just below waist level to allow you to be able to get your upper body weight over the clay. Kneading is more easily accomplished if you utilise your body weight rather than relying on the strength in your arms alone.

Spiral kneading

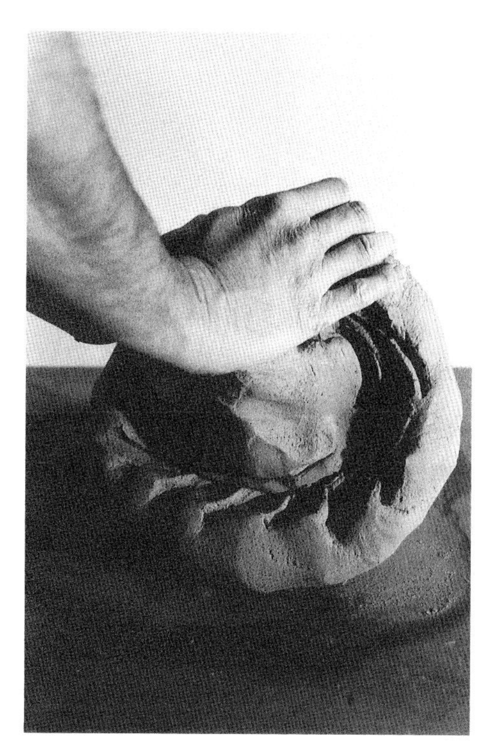

The action of kneading is very difficult to describe but those of you who make your own bread should recognise the process. Begin by taking a weight of clay that you can physically manage, perhaps 5 lb/ 2.25 kg to 10 lb/4.5 kg. The action is to roll the clay to and fro and each time that the clay moves away from you, the heel of your hand pushes down into the clay compressing it against the surface of the wedging table. It is this compression that squeezes the air out. You should hear the air bubbles bursting with an audible 'crack'.

As the clay is pulled back toward the body, the left hand pulls the lump slightly anti-clockwise before the next downward pressure movement. If the whole process has been done correctly the finished lump will retain a definite

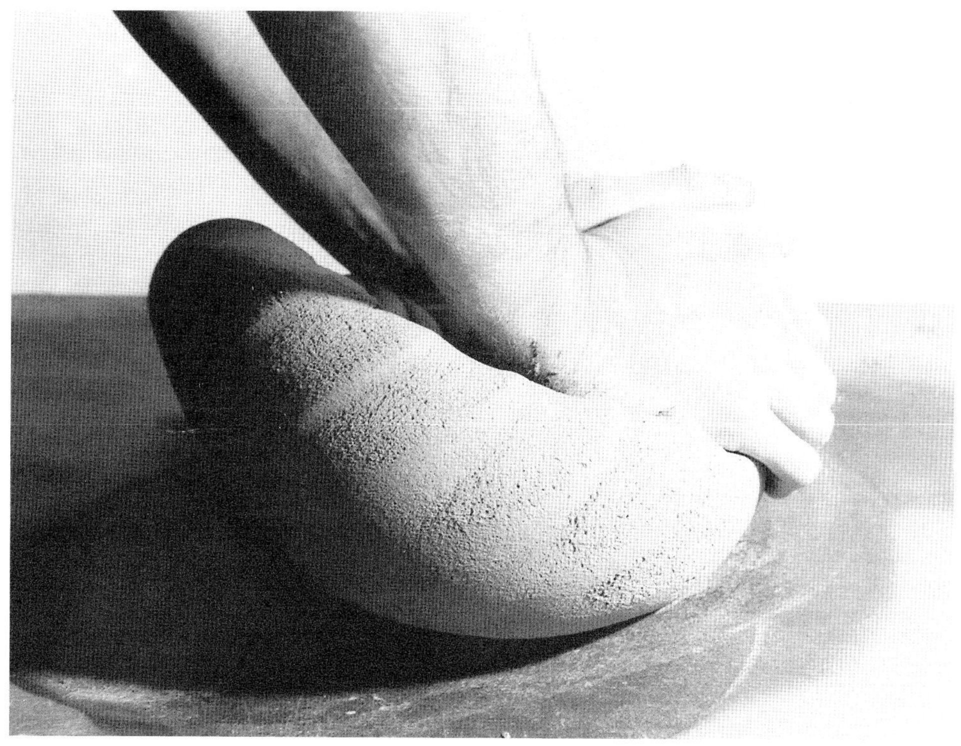

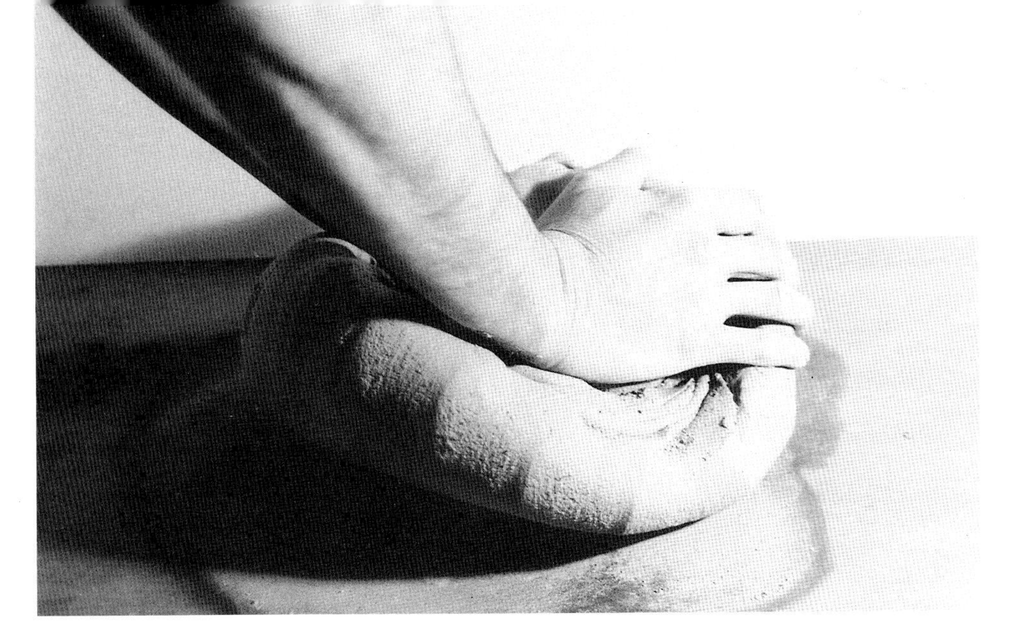

spiral in its shape. Thirty or 40 turns should do the trick but remember ***you must not fold the clay as you push down*** – this will only serve to trap more air.

Kneading is a 'knack' that can be learnt but requires practice. Find a potter that can knead to show you the exact movements, it really isn't as difficult as my description suggests.

Many potters wedge first and then spiral knead afterwards. They believe that the action of spiral kneading begins to align the clay particles that is compounded in the throwing thereby making throwing easier. For myself, I only spiral knead. I find that spiral kneading mixes and de-airs better than any other method and when done properly is also quicker.

In summary

1. *Decide on what type of pottery you wish to make and obtain just one appropriate clay body to begin with, particularly if you have limited space available.*
2. *Try to mix or buy enough clay to last a reasonable length of time. This will give you consistency and allow the clay to improve in storage. Even a ton of plastic clay does not take up a huge space and can be stored out of doors. Remember also that the more you buy at one time, the cheaper it becomes.*
3. *Use your clay in a soft state. It is a mistake to think that if the clay is hard it will last longer on the wheel! The opposite is true. By the time you have struggled to centre a hard lump of clay both you and the clay will be exhausted!*
4. *Be sure that you have prepared your clay for the wheel properly. Hard lumps and air bubbles will frustrate your best efforts.*
5. *If you purchase your clay ready to use from one of the potters' merchants and it is obviously too hard or too soft then complain.*

Chapter Three
Making a Start

A jug by Nigel Lambert, approx. 6 in/5.5 cm tall. Nigel Lambert works in Gloucestershire. His pots are stoneware with a transparent glaze and decorated with cobalt and iron pigments in a free and expressive manner. Nigel is a skilful thrower and his work is often much larger in scale but this little jug is an example of how a simple, un-fussed shape can produce a fine pot when coupled with well thought out and appropriately applied decoration.

There is one more thing that we have to do with the clay before we can begin throwing. You must get into the habit of weighing out your pieces of clay each time you begin work. At the back of the book you will find a table of suggested weights for specific pots as a basic beginner's guide. Eventually you will develop a sense of what weight of clay to use to achieve a certain size of pot but initially you will find it easier to measure your own progress if there is an element of consistency. I would recommend that for your first attempts you weigh out your clay into 1 lb/0.5 kg lumps and carefully pat each lump into an egg shape ready for the wheel. If you have particularly small hands, then perhaps 12 oz/336 g would be enough. Use a wire to neatly cut your prepared and kneaded lump into pieces prior to weighing. If you tear at the clay with your fingers you will only replace the air pockets you have just so carefully and painstakingly removed.

OK. So you have found your clay and you have prepared it for the wheel by wedging it and/or kneading it and you have weighed out a number of 1 lb/0.5 kg smooth, egg-shaped lumps. The big moment has arrived when you sit down at the wheel for the first time. In reality, you will probably do this at an evening class or on a course with a tutor who may have his or her own way of introducing you to the delights of centring. My hope is that you will have read this beforehand and will give my method a try. I am convinced that you will find that in a very short time it will work for you.

Centring

Before we can even begin to make a 'pot' the clay has to be 'centred' on the wheel. The centred lump of clay will revolve as smoothly as the outside edge of the wheelhead itself. It will have no bumps or wobble and be a shape appropriate to the pot that you are about to make. It is relatively easy to detect a wobble in the revolving clay. We can see it and feel it under our fingers. It is though, much more difficult to know when the clay is perfectly centred although I would say that it is as much to do with what you feel through your fingers as it is with sight.

Throwing is very much to do with what you 'feel'. Eventually you will develop very subtle movements with your hands that will achieve certain changes in the pot's shape. It is important that you appreciate the very tactile nature of throwing right from the very beginning. You must learn to coax and to stroke in a gentle and responsive way. Bullying the clay with heavy or jerky movements is to be avoided. Relax and enjoy the process. It is neither a race nor an endurance exercise. When you feel that you have had enough for one day, then leave it. There will be 'off' days, we all have them, when you will begin to wonder why you ever started and buying a pot from a working potter will seem a much easier way out! Console yourself with the thought that centring is the single biggest hurdle to overcome and stick with it.

Never carry on when your patience or energy is exhausted. You will find it easier to resume the next time if you finish on a high note.

Place your bat on the wheel as I have shown you and then slightly dampen,

NOT WET, the surface. With dry hands lightly slap a lump of clay as near to the centre of the bat as you can and then gently pat it with the hand to stick it down and to move it nearer the centre if necessary. Start the wheel at approximately half speed and lift some water with your fingers or a sponge from your bowl onto the revolving clay.

1. Firstly, tense the muscles and tendons in your hands and forearms so that your fingers become rigid and immovable. Your fingers are incredibly strong in this state. Consider how you can carry extremely heavy buckets in one hand just with the fingers crooked around the handle. Well, it is this immense strength that we all possess that is brought to bear in centring.

With your arms securely anchored to either the edge of the splash tray or your legs, lightly place both hands onto the clay. Remember that your hands must act as one, i.e. they will always be touching. With your now rigid fingers, squeeze the heels of your hands toward each other and both hands slightly toward your body until you feel the shape smoothing out and yielding to the inner shape of your hands. At first you may squeeze too hard and the lump will either tear or come off the wheel all together. Don't worry, just put another

lump on the wheel and try again this time with a little less pressure.

During this time you are saying to yourself that the clay will alter its shape to suit your fingers and that your fingers will remain rigid and unyielding. It is at this point you will thank yourself for using soft clay. ***At all times*** relax your grip slowly and gently.

2. *Left* See again how in this second grip the hands are connected and that I am keeping the top of the lump slightly domed. Here, the left hand is containing the clay with inward pressure while the right hand is pushing down. The muscles and tendons are still tensed and it is finger strength combined with a body position that brings the upper body weight over the clay that brings success. The pressure required will lessen as the clay becomes nearer to centre.

3. *Left below* Here you can see that the clay is now perfectly smooth and circular. To the eye and to the touch there is no sign at all of any wobble and we are ready to move on to the next stage of throwing a pot.

4. *Below* It is as well to centre your clay into a shape that is appropriate to the form of the pot that you are about to make. Here, I am centring a flat, wide shape ready to make a shallow dish or perhaps a plate. On page 29 the shape of the centred clay is more suitable for a taller, upright shape such as a jug or vase. Notice here that the hands are still joined together and I am using the heel of my right hand to spread the clay outwards while the left hand is controlling the edge.

In summary

I am not going to try and tell you that centring is easy, it isn't. However, if you remain relaxed and methodical and follow the above rules it won't be long before you master it.

1. *Use* **soft** *clay. You may find that later on as your skills and confidence increase that there will be times when firmer clay is called for in throwing certain shapes e.g. tall jugs or perhaps teapots where a thin wall section is required. Until then use soft clay, it will help you to master movements that will stay with you throughout your potting life.*
2. *Be rhythmical in your movements. A perfectly centred lump will immediately un-centre itself if you remove your hands quickly or indeed if you place your hands on quickly with severe pressure.* ***Always place and remove your hands gradually.***
3. *Use the inherent strength in your tensed fingers to centre for you. If you keep your hands and fingers totally rigid and still then the clay has nowhere to go other than become centred.*
4. *Console yourself in the thought that Hamada, the Japanese potter, rarely began his throwing from a centred lump and look at his pots!*

Salt-glazed bowl by the author, 5 in/12.5 cm tall. See how the lid sits neatly on the rim of the pot with a slight overhang on each side. Without this 'extra' width the lid would appear too small even though it may well physically fit. From this photograph it is also easy to see how the lid has been turned with the overall shape of the finished piece in mind. In fact, the lid was turned using the bowl as a chuck so that the relationship between the shape of the lid to the bowl can be seen constantly as it develops.

Chapter Four
The Two Families of Pots

For the thrower there are two basic 'families' of pots that are within the scope of the potter's wheel. Firstly, there are those forms which are generally taller than they are wide. In this category would be included jugs, mugs, most bottles and vases like the one by Micki Schloessingk illustrated overleaf. The second family are the wider, shallow forms such as bowls, wide dishes and plates.

Both of these 'families' begin with the most basic of pots and present the aspiring thrower with his or her next challenge once centring has been accomplished. The jug by Nigel Lambert on page 23 and Micki Schloessingk's vase illustrated here are perfect examples of how a very basic and relatively simple form can succeed as a beautiful pot providing there is a professional attention to detail and a well thought out and appropriate decoration. A thrown pot need not be a complicated *tour de force*. It is often true in pottery that the simplest answer is the best one and pots of great character and presence can be made with only basic skills if the correct attention is given to maintaining a neat, clean finish right from the very beginning.

A simple cylinder is the 'root' of all the upright, tall forms and can, with only subtle variation, be adapted later on to make the pots that we spoke of earlier. The trick is knowing where to make those subtle deviations from the straight side. But more of that later.

'Going in'

From the centred clay on page 27 and with a slower wheel I have now begun to form the inner space which every vessel has to have. My arms are still securely anchored down and my right hand is placed over the left as a steadying influence. The thumb of my right hand is placed against the outside of the clay and the three middle fingers press down into the pot stopping $\frac{1}{4}$ in/ 7 mm or so before the bat. It is very important that the middle finger is kept exactly in the centre otherwise an unsightly button of clay is left standing at the centre of the base.

Every movement that you make with the clay should be gradual especially when placing or removing your hands. If you take your hands away quickly the clay will immediately become off centre.

A small salt-glazed vase by Micki Schloessingk (UK), 5 in/13 cm high.
Essentially this little vase is a simple cylinder although the gentle inward and outward curves to the form are more difficult to get 'right' than you might expect. Micki Schloessingk's work is noted for its delicate and subtle attention to form yet the finished pots maintain a robust energy and achieve a presence beyond their often modest scale.

'Opening out'

My fingers have reached the bottom of the pot, in this case approximately $\frac{3}{8}$ in/10 mm from the bat's surface, and I am now drawing those fingers outward to meet my thumb on the outside. This movement is slow and rhythmic, never jerky, otherwise your pot will become

off-centred. It is wise to run your fingers back and forth over the base with a firm but not excessive downward pressure. This action consolidates the clay in the base of your pot and will help to avoid cracks appearing in the base as the pot dries.

'Collaring in'

Having achieved a good sharp corner to the base and wall, I now use the whole of my hands to exert gentle *and gradual* pressure inward and over to 'collar' in the entire shape. *Your throwing should always be slightly inward and this movement is the beginning of that. If your pot splays outward too soon you will inevitably lose it or it will prove too difficult to close back in again. So this point is very important indeed.*

'Pulling up'

The 'pulling' of the wall of the pot upward is a difficult movement to master. Start by making a groove at the base of the cylinder. Into this groove place the outside finger while the inside finger fits into the bump immediately above the groove. Exert a modest pinching pressure between the inside and outside fingers. It is this 'bump' that travels up the pot stretching the clay and increasing the height.

Raise your hands in one gentle, easy

movement from the very bottom to a point just below the rim. On reaching the rim allow the pot to turn a few times under your fingers and then remove your hands ***slowly*** so as not to distort the rim. The amount of pressure between the fingers and the speed that your fingers move upwards is something for you to find out by repeated practice. If the pot tears then you were pinching too much. If the pot doesn't grow then you were pinching too little. *Lubricate the pot at regular intervals. If the pot begins to dry then you will notice a dragging effect that can make the pot twist.*

Notice that the hands are still physically connected and acting as one unit.

'Shaping'

I have thrown the cylinder to the height appropriate to the weight of clay that I started with and now I am removing the throwing rings and excess moisture with a throwing rib. Light pressure from the inside with the fingers forces the wall against the straight edged rib, smoothing and consolidating the clay. This consolidation of the pot wall is important, it gives strength to the pot and helps prevent the clay becoming overstretched and liable to collapse.

'Finishing'

Here I am finishing the rim a rounded edge and at the same time consolidating the clay. A soft piece of leather that forms itself into a natural round when folded over is ideal for this. Some potters

recommend the use of chamois leather. I find chamois becomes extremely slimey when wet and difficult to hold onto. Use a soft leather such as that used for a leather jacket.

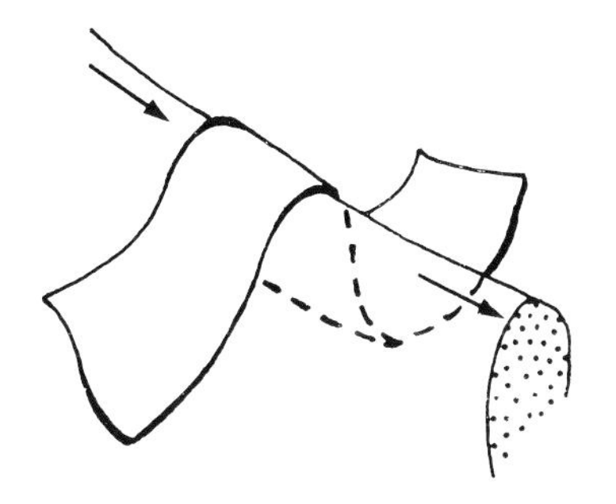

The cylinder is almost complete. I have taken a turning tool with a pointed end to cut a bevel under the outside edge of the base. This bevel acts as a punctuation to the pot at its base whilst at the same time giving the pot a visual sense of lift. The bevel will also serve to keep the glaze away from your kiln shelf when the pot is in the kiln.

Carefully remove the water from the inside of the pot with the sponge stick. If this water is left inside, the pot will almost certainly crack across the base.

'Wiring off'

The cylinder is now complete and I am drawing a wire underneath it. Use a twisted wire that will leave a pleasant pattern to the underneath of the pot. From here the pot can be gently lifted ***with dry hands*** onto a ***clean*** wareboard. Dry your hands on a towel and then gently wrap your hands around the pot and lift. The tacky quality of the surface of the pot will help you to grip the walls without distorting them. Exert only just

enough pressure to allow you to lift the pot but grip and lift with confidence, the more you fiddle and fuss the more of a problem you will find it. Small bowls can also be lifted off but are usually gripped underneath rather than around the sides. If you decide to leave the pot on the throwing bat ***do not*** cut it through at this point but leave it until it can be lifted away comfortably, probably the next day.

A note on the use of lubrication

In the UK we tend to use quite a lot of water during throwing. In the East the opposite is true as it is in the USA. Indeed, in the USA, many of their pottery wheels are sold with little or no splash tray at all. Certainly in Japan lubrication comes from the use of a thick slip rather than water. Water, they feel, leads to pots becoming over wet and ultimately cracking. I tend to use a lot of water, and I get few problems of this sort. It is a fact that one's techniques are to an extent influenced by the materials that we use. If your clay is a 'thirsty' one, that is to say that it takes on rather more water than average, then a slip rather than fresh water may be the answer.

In summary

1. *To begin with, at least, use soft clay.*
2. *Centre with rigid fingers and wrists until confidence allows a more relaxed approach.*
3. *Ensure that the inside base is flat and the right thickness before progressing onto pulling up the walls. If necessary, test the thickness of your base with a needle until you develop an intuitive 'feel' for the correct thickness.*
4. *Lubricate the pot regularly. Use warm water to throw with, especially in winter. Nobody said we have to suffer for our craft!*
5. *Use gentle, rhythmic movements.* ***Never*** *bully the clay.* ***Always lay your hands on or take them off gradually.***
6. *Always take care to achieve a professional finish to your pot. Pay attention to the rim, leave it rounded and smooth, avoid sharp edges. Always use a clean wareboard. Use clean dry hands when lifting your pots.*

This small vase by Shoji Hamada is another example of the basic cylinder shape with only very subtle variation in line. The rich black tenmoku glaze has been wiped away with the fingers to create a spontaneous and lively pattern.

The bowl

The second family of pots are the wide, shallow forms such as bowls, dishes and plates. Small bowls are probably the easiest forms to throw and beginners often find that a bowl is the first 'pot' that they make. Larger bowls and plates present difficulties in control in that the centrifugal force of the spinning wheel encourages the wide shallow form to collapse at the edge where the wheel is travelling faster than at the centre. Work your way up to these larger pieces gradually.

A bowl by Peter Beard (UK), 9 in/23 cm diameter.
Peter Beard uses a combination of glaze and wax resist to 'construct' a highly textured and patterned surface on his pots. This bowl shows very well the smooth, uninterrupted curve from one rim to the other that a well-thrown bowl should contain.

1. I have centred the clay in the same way as I did for the cylinder and my fingers go down through the middle to form a hollow as before. The difference here is that in this case instead of forming a flat base my thumb and forefinger extend the clay outwards leaving the inside of the hollow curved rather than flat.

2. I slow the wheel a little. Here the thumb and forefinger continue to extend the clay outwards and upwards by a pinching and pulling movement being careful to leave the inside with a rounded curve. Notice how the other hand is steadying the rim and helping to control any tendency to overstretch the clay.

3. This is the final pull. As I come to the rim with my fingers pinching lightly, I will have achieved the size of bowl that I wanted. I am still very concerned to keep the inside a good flowing curve right through the bowl from rim to rim. ***Do not over thin the wall of the bowl at this stage.***

4. Here I use a throwing rib to smooth out the inside contour of the bowl. Allow the natural curve of the rib to do the work for you. Use as much of the curve as you can whilst all the time using the fingers of the outside hand to give inward support against the rib. It is surprising how much pressure can be exerted with the rib as long as it is met

with equal pressure from outside the bowl. ***A curved throwing rib similar to the one pictured here is essential for the throwing of bowls.***

5. Bowls can be made with either a flat underside as in the one on the left or, as on the right, with a thicker base to allow for a footring to be 'turned' underneath. Be generous with the thickness if you intend a footring.

6. In this case I have shaved away some of the waste clay around the bottom of the bowl and I have wired it through. Now, with clean, dry hands I am able to lift it from the wheelhead and on to a wareboard.

7. With most of my pots I try to take them from the wheel as near to finished as possible. Here I am cutting away even more surplus clay from underneath, ready for the bowl to receive its footring. This clay has served its purpose in that it

has provided support during the throwing. Now, it can disappear while the clay is soft and the cutting is effortless.

In summary

1. *Take time to ensure that you have a flowing curve within your bowl. A beginner's bowl will often have an unsightly bump in its contour (see diagram). This happens when the bowl begins to sag over the edge of its own base. Practice in the use of the rib and a generous diameter to the base will overcome this.*

This diagram shows the most common fault in a beginner's thrown bowl. The clay has been allowed to sag over the edge of the base which produces an unsightly bump in the internal curve. Use of a curved rib together with a generous amount of clay to act as a support will overcome this.

2. *Be generous with the thickness of the base if you intend your bowl to have a footring.*

   Later in the book, as we look at turning, I will discuss the form and proportions of the bowl and the huge differences that can be imposed on the character of a bowl by subtle differences in the proportion and shape of the footring.

'Good pots'

Once you can throw a cylinder and a simple bowl shape with reasonable fluency then it is time to move on and try to expand your repertoire. Anything that you try to make from now on has its roots in what you have already accomplished. Larger, taller and wider pots will present new problems to overcome but practice, as always, is the key.

Throwing pots is a lot like playing a musical instrument. There are scales to be learnt and there is constant, hopefully daily practice before anything like a professional fluency appears. Unfortunately, the ability to throw a piece of clay into a tall cylinder or wide dish is only half the battle. Knowing ***what*** to make and the ***'right'*** shape to make it is the other half. Make a pact with yourself right from the very beginning that you will not accept any pot that you can see to be a bad form. Look upon your failures as stepping stones to successes, seek out and examine exemplary pots and you will quickly begin to recognise a good shape in your own work.

I cannot stress enough the importance of experiencing hand-thrown pots, both historical and contemporary, before you begin throwing and throughout your pottery career. I have a number of pots by other potters around my house and I gain huge enjoyment and inspiration from having them around me. Unfortunately, too many people come to pottery unaware of the rich and varied traditions that lie within it. It is a mistake to begin making pots with nothing more than industrial crockery as your total ceramic 'experience'. The making of hand-thrown pottery as compared to industrially-made ceramics, contains an entirely different set of aesthetic standards as to what constitutes a successful pot. Using the bland, anonymous industrially-made pot as a benchmark for your own successes or failures is misleading and entirely the wrong thing to do.

There are now many museums that have collections of both historical and contemporary pots. There are even one or two collections that allow you to handle certain pots. Visit good quality craft 'galleries' and try to decide which of the many and varied pots that are on offer appeal to you most. Absorb, as much as you can, the qualities of the hand-thrown pot. Study their different structural parts, the base, the footring, the handle, the weight and the thickness. Make drawings of historical pots that you admire. There is no better way, however good or bad your drawing, of imprinting a particularly good form on the memory.

Pouring bowl by Lee Kang Hyo, Korea, 7 in/18 cm diam.
Lee Kang Hyo works with very soft clay and a traditional Korean momentum wheel that is little more than a wooden turntable mounted in the earth floor that requires constant kicking. The slow wheel speed and the soft clay combined with skill and confidence creates pots with great energy and life. The brushed slip or 'hakame' decoration, a traditional Korean technique, further adds to the feeling of movement.

In short, there is little use in learning the skills of the thrower if you have little idea of what to do with those skills. There are many decisions to be made each time you throw a new pot. Decisions, for example, as to the height in relation to the width or the diameter. Where should the fattest part be? What is the relationship of the neck of a jug to its handle? How does the height of a pot affect its girth? Why does the shape and direction of a footring affect so much the overall character of a bowl?

All of these questions and many more are often overlooked in books of this type and yet without, at least, some of the answers you will not make thrown pots of real quality.

There are many, many ways of orchestrating, let's say, a jug so that it functions well and looks visually pleasing. Unfortunately, it is also true that there are just as many ways, probably even more, of achieving the opposite. We have to learn to be able to recognise the good from the bad and know why. We can only achieve this by constant observation and handling of the best of hand-thrown pottery.

From this point on we shall look at the throwing of very specific pots. I shall try to show you not only the practical considerations in the making, many of the techniques are common to other pots, but give you some aesthetic guidelines that should set you on the right track for your own personal development.

Chapter Five
The Jug

The jug or pitcher is a peculiarly European concept. In the Orient, the jug as we Westerners understand it did not really exist until Bernard Leach introduced it to Hamada who in turn took the form back to Japan in the mid 1920s. Leach based many, if not all, his own jugs on the medieval ideal and felt that 'no pots, save the Chinese, possess such a warmth and vigour'. There have been two books above all others that have had the greatest impact on the studio potters of this country. One is Leach's own book, *The Potter's Book* and the other is Bernard Rackham's *Medieval English Pottery* which consists almost entirely of jugs. *Medieval English Pottery* is almost essential reading for any aspiring or even practising potter although it is now a collector's item and very difficult to find. Try your local library or perhaps seek it out in secondhand bookshops. Hamada became fascinated by the variety of form and the honest, direct qualities of the medieval European jug and, in particular, English examples and continued to make medieval inspired jugs until his death.

In contemporary studio pottery the jug still retains a universal interest for potters. Many continue to find new and personal re-interpretations of the medieval pitcher, while in recent years a new breed of ceramic 'makers' have taken the jug form and certain ideas about its often rather ceremonial nature and created avant-garde ceramic sculpture in 'homage' to its importance as a fundamental pottery icon.

A tall faceted jug by Jim Malone (UK).
The edges of the cut facets in this jug emphasise its elongated shape. Jim Malone has taken the essential qualities of the medieval jug and combined it with some of the making features of the Oriental potter to create a new interpretation of a traditional pot. There is detailed orchestration here. It is no coincidence that the handle begins from a pronounced ridge or that it rejoins the pot on a subtle shoulder. These are features that you must plan for your pots and the sort of questions that you must be asking yourself as you work.

In the opening section to this book I told you that there are two families of pots. The jug is, in its simplest form, a short step forward from the cylinder that we have already looked at. We need only to make subtle alterations to the outside profile to make a perfectly acceptable jug. It is, of course, extremely important, however little your shape differs from the straight-sided cylinder, that all the elements of your form are assembled in a harmonious whole.

A jug, like a teapot, requires a balance to be struck between parts of the pot that either protrude from the symmetrical, the lip, or which have to be added on, the handle. You will see in the jug we are about to make that I begin with a cylinder and my form grows from within it.

A tall salt-glazed jug by the author, 14 in/35.5 cm tall. This jug has its roots firmly in the medieval European tradition both in its form and glazed surface. Salt-glazing began in Germany during the late medieval period and became a popular method of glazing pottery for industrial purposes in England from the 16th century well into the 20th century.

1. I have centred the clay and made one 'pull'. Here I am halfway through the second pull. My outside fingers are underneath the bulge and on the inside my middle finger is inside the bulge. The position of the fingers creates a wave motion in the clay and it is this 'wave' that travels up the pot stretching the clay as it goes.

Note that I am throwing slightly toward the centre of the wheel.

This action will help to keep the rim narrower than the diameter of the base. It is very difficult to make a wide opening significantly narrower. It is relatively easy to increase the opening when and if you need to.

2. I had achieved a cylinder exactly like the one on page 32 and now I am beginning to form a swelling by gentle pressure with the inside fingers while using the outside fingers to guide and control the amount of swelling. Notice that the swelling does *not* begin at the very bottom of the pot wall. There is a fairly straight line that moves upward from the bat into the swelling. This is

easier to see in the photograph on p. 41. It is this line that gives the jug its visual lift and prevents the final shape from looking bottom heavy or dumpy.

3. Here, I am 'collaring' in the middle section. Collaring is a light 'strangulation' movement while at the same time moving the hands slowly upward.

I have thought about the orchestration of the finished jug and in particular the joining of the handle. I have made the very top of the pot curve inwards and it is from here that the handle will start. It seems appropriate that the handle will finish on the widest part of the belly thus enclosing the inward curve and hopefully creating a pleasant shape between handle and pot. Leave a rounded and generous thickness to the rim. A very thin edge is unsightly and will chip easily.

4. I am refining the shape with a throwing rib. Notice again how I am steadying the rib with the thumb of the other hand. Satisfied with the shape of the curve, I have used the rib to define a 'soft' edge to the rim and purposely left the marks of the rib behind in the body of the jug. I find that this kind of expressive throwing suits the glazes that I use and may not be appropriate to all glazes and decorations.

Three jugs by Svend Bayer (UK), roller decorated, tallest 14 in/36 cm tall.
Svend Bayer has his pottery in North Devon and is renowned as a consummate thrower of a very wide range of domestic pots including enormous planters. The kiln is wood-fired and many of the pots rely on Svend's experience and knowledge of his kiln to take advantage of the fly ash from the fires to create the wonderful surfaces.

These jugs are, by any standards, large pots, they are well thrown and are not physically heavy for their size. Yet, because of the careful attention to details such as the relationship of the 'belly' to the diameter of the base and the line of growth from the base upwards, they remain ***visually*** 'light' also. It would be very easy to mismanage these important lines and create a heavy or clumsy appearance.
Photograph by Thomas Dobbie.

5. The body of the jug is now complete and all that remains to do is to cut a chamfer underneath the bottom edge. ***Two hands*** on the cutting tool.

6. Your jug will require a pouring lip. I do not like vulgar overstatement in pottery. Details such as pouring lips should, in my opinion, sit quietly and correctly within the overall scheme of things rather than be an eye catching and distracting 'feature'. Here, I am using the thumb and forefinger of my left hand to hold back the edge of the rim as the forefinger of the right hand forms the lip with a side to side movement while at the same time exerting a downward pressure.

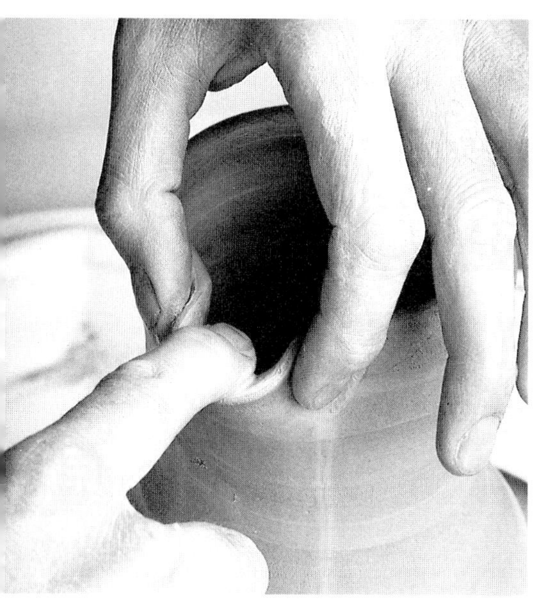

7. The lip now needs to be pulled back toward the centre both to make sure that it is straight and to bring the rim of the jug back to a circle. The lip should be an extension on the edge of a circle rather than the rim of your jug taking on a vastly over-exaggerated 'pear' shape to accommodate the lip.

In summary

1. *Until your confidence increases, begin by achieving a cylinder and then move on to finding your shape.*

2. *Be mindful of your finished shape before you start. I firmly believe that you should always know exactly the shape you want to achieve before you begin throwing. However, I also believe that if you make a* **good** *pot that isn't exactly what you had in mind, there's no reason on earth why you shouldn't accept it and pat yourself on the back for recognising a successful shape. Throwing should be fun, sometimes a fortuitous accident can lead to a new series of ideas.*

3. *When making the pouring lip, use clean but wet hands.*

Handles

Having just looked at the making of the body of a jug, it seems appropriate here to take a break from throwing and look at the making of a pulled handle.

There are a number of ways of making handles for your pots. An extruder or 'wad box' is a very basic and simple machine that squeezes clay through a pre-cut die. The die is cut to the cross-sectional shape of the handle required and the resulting strips are merely cut into appropriate lengths and applied to the pot. A similar type of handle can be made by dragging a pre-formed loop of wire through a block of clay. You can even roll a handle much in the same way that you would roll a coil. They can be pressed from a mould or cut from a flat slab and then either impressed or combed to produce a pattern for character and interest. Handles can even be thrown, as a whole piece like the saucepan handle to a teapot or casserole, or cut into sections to form an arc or a loop. As usual in ceramics, the only limit to potential is your own imagination. Certainly the handle in all its forms has great potential for imaginative variation and thereby an opportunity for imparting your own personal 'style' to your pots.

Two alternative ways of making a handle

Figure 1 shows an extruder or 'wad box'. Clay is forced through a pre-cut die and emerges as a handle section much like a sausage from a sausage machine. Figure 2 is a cutter, much used in the 19th century in the production of utility wares, that is dragged through a solid block of clay. Peel back the clay and reveal the handle section inside. In my opinion, neither of these methods will produce the spontaneous vitality of a well-pulled and joined handle but may have their place in making a particular kind of pot.

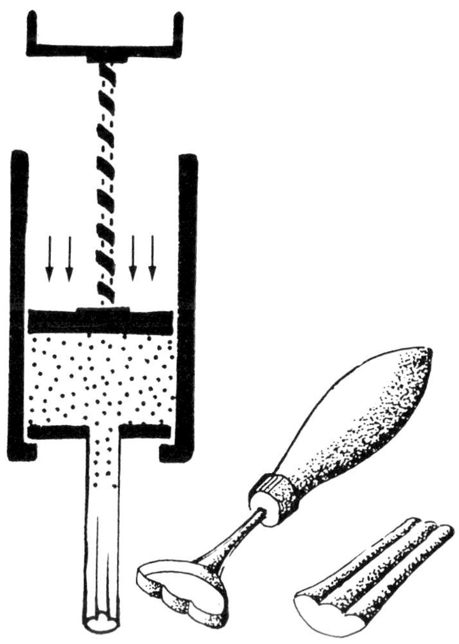

Two salt-glazed jugs by Sarah Walton, (UK), $8\frac{1}{2}$ in/21.5 cm tall.

These two jugs have a monumental presence that belies their modest scale. Even though the forms are quite precisely thrown and extreme in their bulbous nature, the jugs retain a softness of line that seems to emphasise the distended feel to the body. The ends of the handles are fine examples of how the point of attachment should grow out of the pot, gradually lending strength to the joint.

I firmly believe though, that any thrower worthy of the craft should be able to 'pull' a handle. Handle pulling is as much an integral part of throwing a pot as the forming of a pouring lip or the turning of a footring. Unfortunately, the bad news is that the pulling of handles is almost as difficult to master as the throwing of the pot itself and requires much practice. I told you in the Introduction that I intend you to use this book in conjunction with good quality tuition. Nowhere is that more true than at this point. Handle pulling is a true skill and you will need someone to show you at least once or twice before you try it for yourself.

Cathi Jefferson, Canada.

Brigitte Pénicaud, France.

There is no such thing as a standard handle. The shape, length, weight, cross section will vary from jug to jug or mug to mug. As you can see from the above photographs the line of the handle differs greatly according to the form of the pot. A taller, slender shape usually requires that the handle stays closer to the body throughout its length while a fatter, rounder shape will often take a handle that springs out in a wider curve. As with most things in pottery, there are no definitive rules and often a decision as to what looks best while at the same time functioning well is your responsibility.

Phil Rogers.

This is the jug that we made in the previous section. It is now firm enough to handle without damage. Before we even begin the handle, I want to show you how I deal with the bottom edge.

All pots which have a flat base i.e. one that does not require turning as part of the overall shape should be left alone. There is no better way to finish the underneath of a jug for instance, than to leave a fresh, clean, unmarked wire pattern on the base. Here, I am wiping my thumb carefully around the outer edge and allowing the natural curve that is created by the soft pad of the thumb to make a neat, rounded edge.

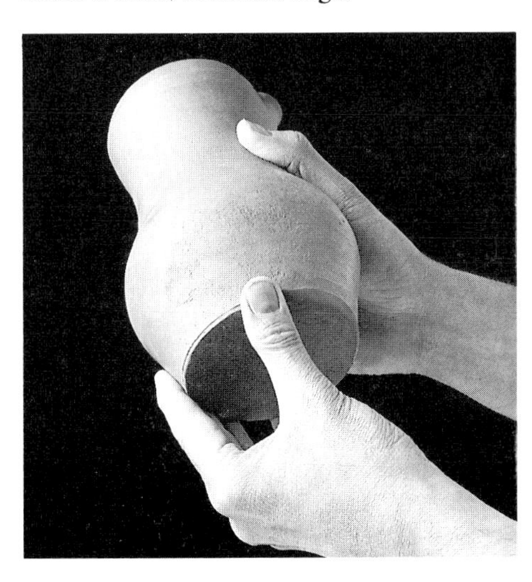

A small salt-glazed jug by the Author, 6 in/ 15.5 cm tall.

This small jug was first thrown as a cylinder and then the 'lattice' pattern was applied by hitting the pot with a carved wooden paddle that imprinted the design. A hand is held inside to lend some support as the wall is 'hit'. The pot was then swollen from the inside with gentle outward pressure and finished in the usual way.

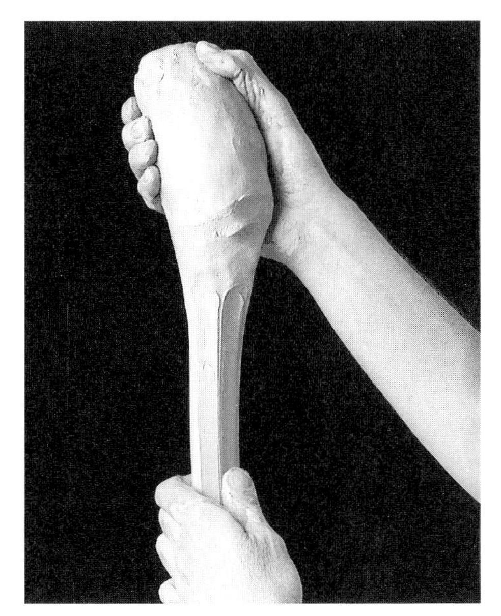

I pull my handles in two stages. The handle is pulled partially from a fairly large lump and finished with more pulling after it is attached to the pot.

Roughly fashion a lump of clay that is big enough to supply a number of handles and a size that you can comfortably grip in one hand. Begin by patting the clay into the shape that we have here and then wet the lower portion. The idea is to pull and stroke the clay, with a light pinching pressure, downwards allowing gravity to help you. A pull begins at the very top and continues until your hand comes off the end. With each pull the handle should increase in length. Pull in rhythmic, easy movements, never stopping halfway. Keep the clay wet but 'feel' for that light pinch that s-t-r-e-t-c-h-e-s the clay.

The handle is getting longer and here you can see that I am keeping the whole thing symmetrical by working on both sides equally. My thumb is beginning to create a ridge down the centre which will eventually become a feature of the handle. Notice how my fingers are hooked around the outside of the clay so as to prevent the handle from moving to the side as I stroke it downward.

As each handle or 'plug' is as finished as we need it at this stage, I lay it down on a table and use my thumb to cut it off from the main lump. It is important never to allow the handle to bend severely, this will cause a thinning and weakness at that point.

Before you begin a session of handle making, you will need to organise your workspace carefully. You will need a towel within easy reach, a bench wheel, a soft sponge and a potter's knife. You will also need a free, ***clean*** and uncluttered table or wareboard to set down the finished pots.

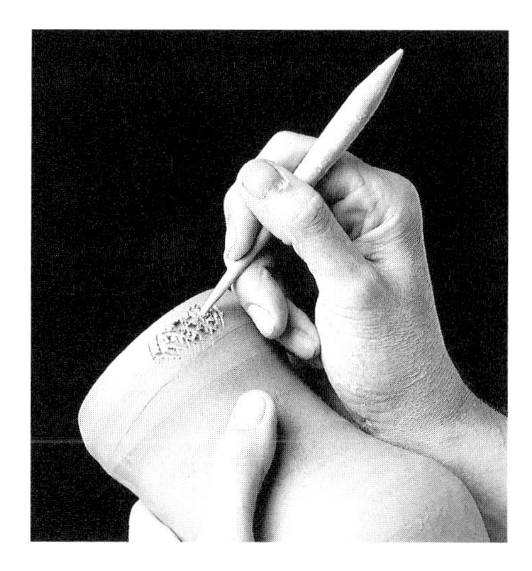

As I come to each new pot I pick up a 'plug' and tap the end flat with my finger while holding it lightly between the fingers of the other hand. This forms a slight mushroom effect which you can emphasise by a light pinching out.

Lightly score the area that will take the handle both at the top and the bottom and dab on a small amount of sticky slurry. **Not water**. You can also score the end of the handle to match.

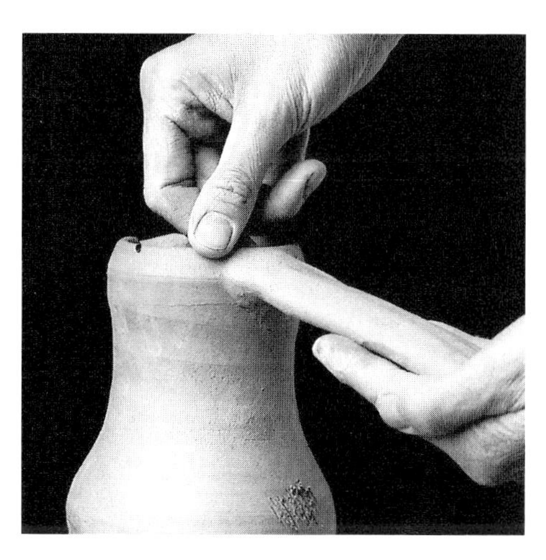

The handle is now pushed firmly into place using the ***whole*** of its length and ***all*** of your hand. If you apply too much pressure at any one point, you will cause a thin weak area. Mould the joint all the way around and completely seal the edge with your finger. If your handle comes off during the next stage, it is likely that you have not made a perfect seal all around the joint.

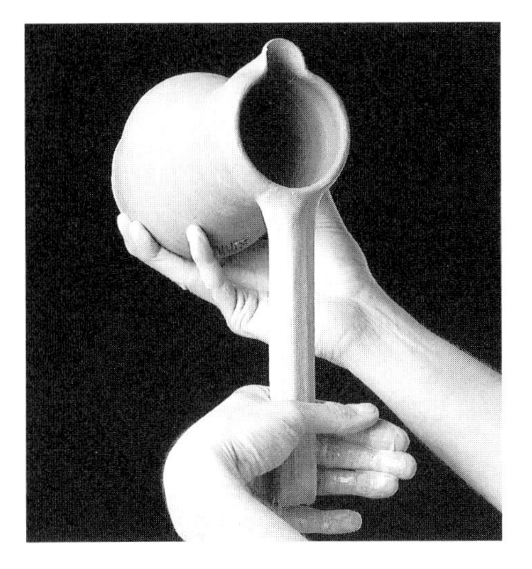

Pick up the jug always supporting the handle and not allowing it to bend at all. Hold the jug so that the handle hangs down and continue to pull it in the same way that you were earlier.

Notice that the holding hand is ***clean*** and not covered in slip.

Keep the pulling hand and the handle itself well-lubricated.

I have decided that I have pulled and extended the handle so that it is now the right weight and scale for the size of the jug. I have achieved an 'eye' shaped cross-sectional shape. A flat square edge will make your handle look thick and heavy from the side.

Here, I am using my thumb nail to 'drag' two grooves as a decorative feature. My fingers wrapped around the outside act as a guide and help me to pull in a straight line.

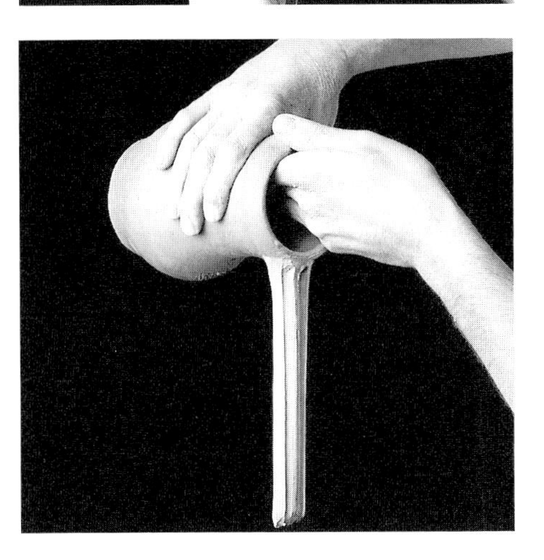

Before I can attach the handle at the bottom end I need to change my grip on the jug. With clean hands (the towel is close by you, or it should be!), I take hold of the body of the jug with my right hand making sure that the handle always hangs straight down and does not bend.

I take hold of the handle and hold it straight. ***It is the jug that moves to meet the handle***. Bring the bottom of the jug around to meet the handle.

Attach the handle at the point that you have scored, and pinch off and discard any surplus length. Before you secure the handle, firmly just check, by looking down on the pot, that you have the handle straight and that it is directly in line with the lip.

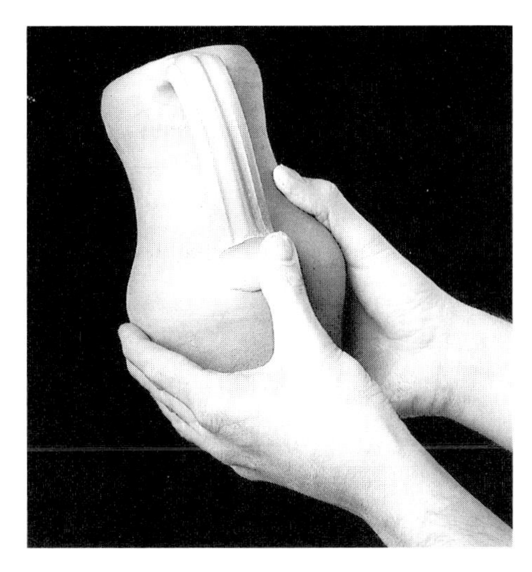

There are a number of ways to add a finishing touch to the end of a handle. I have formed the clay into a rounded end and then with a side to side motion I flatten and join the handle to the pot always keeping the joint symmetrical. In finishing the handle we have an opportunity for introducing an element of individuality. It is often details such as a particular handle cross-section or the way in which a handle is terminated that helps to mark your pot out from other people's.

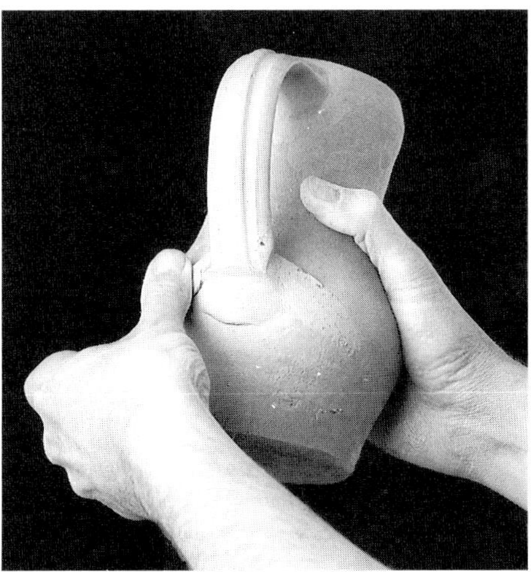

The finished handle. The last thing that I have done is to insert a small 'sausage' of clay into the gap in the bottom joint and smooth it in to form a curved transition from pot to handle. The photograph above shows you how I thumb off the ends of the sausage blending them into the jug. It is important that your handle should have a smooth, continuous curve. It should also grow from your pot much in the way that your arm 'grows' from your shoulder, a natural, flowing joint. Try not to destroy the natural curve of the clay by over-touching with a heavy hand but minor adjustments to the curve can be made on the inside with a wet finger.

Two salt-glazed pitchers by the Author, tallest 18 in/46 cm high.

The tall, slender shape of these two pitchers seems to dictate that the handle stays quite close to the body of the pot rather than springing out in a wide curve. You will need to consider questions of this kind as you throw your pots. Looking, handling and drawing many, many pots will help you to come to understand good form and appropriate orchestration.

Left

The finished jug.

Chapter Six
A Plate

A small plate is probably the single most uncomplicated item that a potter is called upon to make. Of course, as the size of the plate increases so the problems multiply also, but this is true of all pots and is overcome with practice and a gradual increase in scale rather than being over-ambitious too soon which can lead to frustration. I strongly recommend that you throw all your plates on a bat so that they can be lifted off without any risk of distortion.

The first sequence of photographs shows the making of a small and simple flat-bottomed plate which will require no turning except a small bevel done at a later stage. It is the kind of basic domestic item that could be called a teaplate. This plate is very low in height and can be fired in the kiln packed in columns or 'bungs' of small kiln shelves rather than spread uneconomically over large shelves.

Tea plates stacked on small kiln shelves with three spacers set at the two corners and one in the middle of the opposite edge. Stacking plates this way can save a great deal of space in your kiln, making firing much more economical.

Here I have centred the clay wide and low as I would in preparation for any plate or wide shallow form. Exert as much controlled pressure down onto the clay as you can. All wide, shallow items are prone to cracking across the base so you must consolidate the clay against the bat while you have the chance.

Slow the wheel down.

With my thumb and forefinger I have lifted the clay at the outside edge to create a thick, rounded 'doughnut' like

shape. Then, with light pinching pressure I am beginning to flatten the rim while at the same time there is a gentle easing outwards. The thickness of the plate here will be its finished thickness. Be generous, a plate that is wafer-thin across its base will either crack or 'hump' i.e. the base will rise up in the kiln much like the top of a fruitcake.

The rim has now been formed between thumb and forefinger and the plate is now almost complete and only requires definition to the form.

Here I am using a throwing rib to shape the 'well' of the plate by allowing the curve of the rib to form the transition from well to rim and then, with the support of my fingers underneath, to smooth down and flatten the rim.

Right
A large platter by David Frith (UK), 20 in/ 51 cm across.
David Frith works with his wife, Margaret, in North Wales. He is well-known as an accomplished thrower of large and often very complicated forms. This large plate has been glazed firstly with a celadon and then overglazed with a *kaki*. The edge of the rim has been carved in the leatherhard state.

Pay particular attention to the relationship of the width of the 'rim' to that of the diameter of the inner 'well'. There is a 'rightness' here which is well worth noting.

The finished plate is lifted from the wheel still attached to the bat. I will wire it through when it has firmed up a little. I have introduced a swirl to the well of the plate as a decorative feature. This is done with the edge of throwing rib with a deft and confident movement from the outer edge toward the middle.

This plate now only requires minimal turning to the very edge of the base to finish it. The underneath remains flat and ***clean***, free from fingermarks or crumbs of dry clay.

In this second series of photographs I am making a rather larger plate or dish that might serve food at the dining table or could even be a fruit bowl.

The problem that you are likely to encounter here is that the extra weight of clay and the increased diameter will encourage the clay to 'slump' down at the edge. Once you have centred the clay, ***slow the wheel down***. The wheel will be travelling much faster at the edge than the centre so beware. Also, it is important to leave a generous diameter to the underneath of your plate while you are throwing it. This extra clay acts as a support to the edge and can be cut away later during the turning.

The clay is centred low and wide. I use the heel of my hand to spread the clay across the wheelhead.

With the wheel a little slower, I am using the natural curve of my hand to begin the 'dish' shape by pressing harder at the centre and slowly releasing the pressure as my hand reaches the outer edge. My thumb on the left hand is at the outer edge next to the bat pushing inwards to prevent any further spread.

The thick edge that you can see in the figure on page 57 has been pulled upward in much the same way as the bowl on page 36. The wheel is now travelling quite slowly.

Here I am smoothing and forming a continuous and gentle curve to the well of the plate before flattening and defining the rim as I previously did (p. 54). You will notice here that I have not folded the rim to make the outer flange. Instead I have pulled it out from the thickness at the edge (see diagram). To fold the rim is to build into your plate a weakness and it is at this point that the plate will tend to collapse. ***Slow wheel***.

The plate has been completed and here I emphasise the change from the 'well' to the 'rim' by incising a line. The glazes that I use require lines and marks in the clay so that they can run and pool to highlight these areas. Another potter may choose to place this same line of emphasis as a band of colour within the glaze. I am using a chisel-ended tool to make a broad, indented line that begins thinly, becomes stronger and broader and then thins again as it reaches its end.

A final smoothing away of throwing marks that would otherwise interfere with any subsequent decoration.

The finished article. I have decorated the centre of the plate by drawing into the

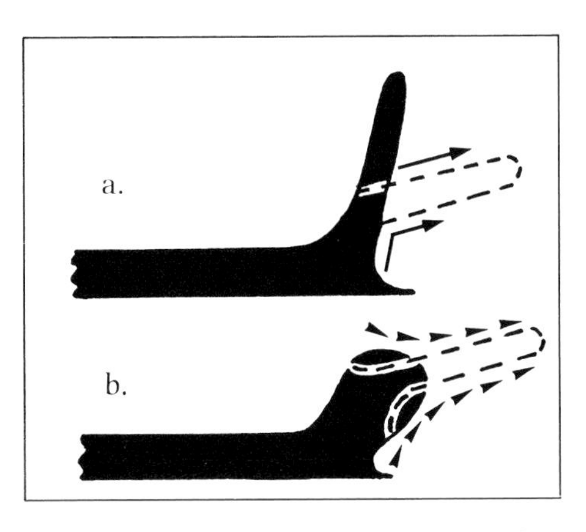

Figure (a) shows the wrong way to make the outer flange of a plate. A fold like this will create a weakness and the plate is likely to collapse. Figure (b) shows the correct way. Pull the flange out of a thick edge so as not to fold or crease the clay.

clay with the sharp corner of a wooden tool. The inner circle which is broken by the drawing acts as a frame to the motif.

This plate now requires a footring turned onto the back. I can only do this once the plate has become firmer so I leave it on the bat until the next day when I will wire it through. It is a good idea to dry plates and wide dishes standing on their rims on a perfectly flat, *clean* board. You will find that there is much less tendency for the rims to distort by this method.

You will see this plate turned and finished later in the book.

In summary

1. *Centre the clay wide and low. The diameter of the centred clay is equal to the width of the base of the plate during the throwing, so don't underestimate the width required for support.*
2. *Slow the wheel down as soon as you have finished centring. When you are working on the rim, the wheel is very slow indeed.*
3. *Pull the rim of the plate out of a thick 'doughnut' like edge.* ***DO NOT fold the clay to make the rim.***
4. *Pay attention to the relationship of scale between the width of the rim or flange and the diameter of the well.*
5. *If your plate is to be turned later, be sure to leave enough of a thickness at the centre to allow for the type of footring that you want.*
6. *Finish the edge of your plate with the leather to round it over and to consolidate the clay. There is a risk of small cracks appearing in the rim if this isn't done.* ***There is little point in finishing the edge of the plate with a leather in a professional manner only to put the plate on its rim to dry onto a dirty, dusty surface.***

Chapter Seven
Bottles

The bottle has always been of fundamental concern to the potter. Initially, the bellied shape that closed over at the top usually with a neck, was used for storage or as a container in which liquids could be sold from one person to another. Later, and primarily in the East, the bottle form became a vase, a decorative and often ceremonial vessel that became the standard, above all other forms, as the finest work that the potter could produce. In the West, bottles were produced as early as the 13th century but their purpose was

Late 18th-century salt-glazed bottle, 5 in/ 12.5 cm tall.
This small bottle was made in London. The speed and energy of the throwing is still there to be seen as a spiralling movement upwards imprinted in the clay's surface.

almost certainly utilitarian. To make vases merely to be ornamental is an idea that does not seem to have occurred to the medieval potter. Take a look at, amongst others, the bottles and vases of Yi Dynasty Korea and Sui, Tang and Sung Dynasty China as well as more recent studio pots.

I am going to show you two bottle forms. One is very basic indeed and the other a little more complicated, a kind of throwing 'trickery' that you can try as your skills and confidence increase. Most potters like to make bottles that either function in the kitchen as pouring or storage vessels or forms that are really vases and have a more decorative or contemplative function. Either way the problems involved in throwing the bottle shape are the same.

It is little wonder considering the rather anthropomorphic nature of the bottle that we refer to its different parts in human terms. Indeed, the most difficult part of throwing any kind of bottle is the 'collaring' in of the 'neck' after you have finished forming the bulbous 'body' or 'belly' below it. Like the human form, we have to give consideration as to how each of these elements 'grows' into one another. Lines of growth and change must be handled with grace and subtlety, particularly at those points where curves change from concave to convex or vice versa such as at the 'shoulder' or near the 'foot'.

A common mistake is to believe that the 'belly' of the bottle must be completely finished before the neck is closed over. This is not quite true. First, there is the 'throwing stick' that can be used as an extra long 'finger' to swell out a pot and secondly, a certain amount of refinement of shape can be done with a throwing rib from the outside even when the bottle is almost finished.

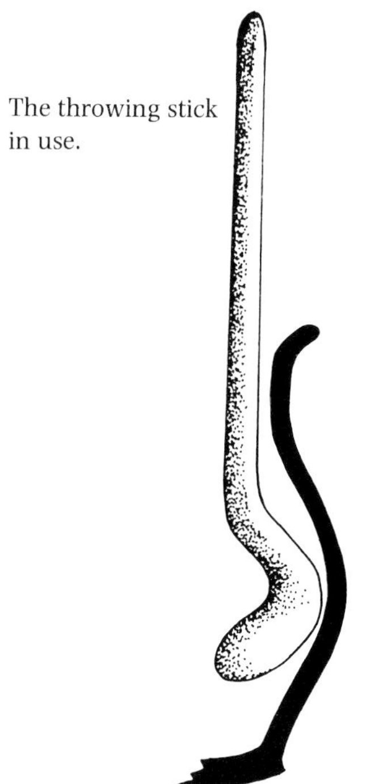

The throwing stick in use.

I have centred the clay in the usual way and begun to pull up the walls into a cylinder.

Think of your cylinder as $\frac{2}{3}$ for the belly or body of the bottle and $\frac{1}{3}$ for the shoulder, neck and rim. The most common mistake in throwing bottles is not to leave enough clay for the upper parts. It is better to have a little too

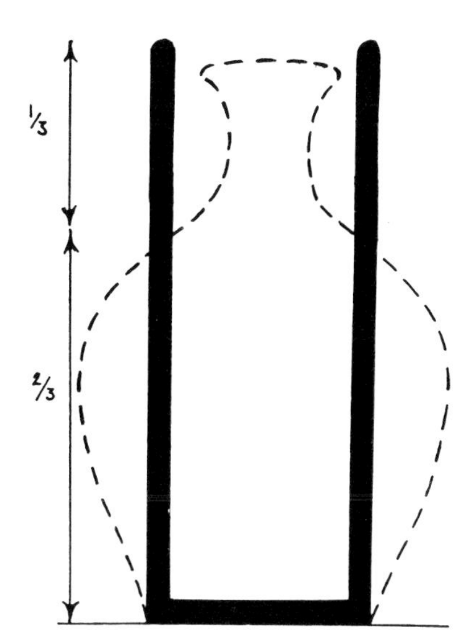

Drawing of cylinder with 1/3 : 2/3 proportions.

much rather than trying to finish the neck and rim with too little clay. The result will look thin and mean.

Gentle outward pressure from the inside is controlled with the outside fingers to form the rounded shape. As the fingers rise toward the shoulder the outside fingers are positioned slightly above the inside and inward pressure at this point completes the 'belly'.

Collaring in the neck. Collaring is a movement that you will need to practice as it is impossible to describe the tendency for the clay to sink or ripple

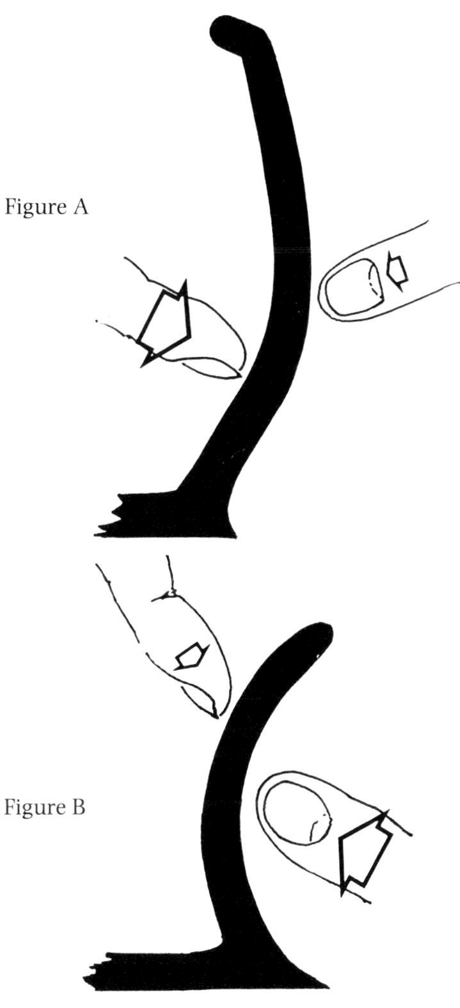

In Figure A the fingers are positioned so as to induce an outward curve to the wall of the pot and in Figure B an inward curve. The size of the arrows are indicative of the relative pressures involved. The fingers with the smaller arrows are supporting and controlling while the larger arrows are forming the shape. Bear in mind that the fingers are rising up the pot wall as this is happening and this shaping process is often a delicate rather than forceful movement.

when put under this pressure to reduce its diameter. This is something that you have to 'feel' before you can begin to know how to position the fingers in an effective way. As with nearly every facet of pottery there is no absolute rule. The most effective and comfortable finger positions may be different for you and that is OK. All I can do is show you what works for me and leave it up to you to decide for yourself.

The fingers are arranged around the pot in such a way so that there is the maximum amount of contact between skin and clay. The fingers exert a pressure inwards and at the same time upwards in a kind of stroking action. Each time a collaring movement is made you will find that the wall of the pot thickens slightly as you reduce its diameter. You can then carefully pull the clay up to extend the height of the wall and then go back to collaring. ***Be careful not to push downward, as there is a tendency for a shoulder to collapse as you collar in.***

I am putting the final, delicate touches to the neck and rim.

In this larger and slightly more complicated bottle below the basic rules that we have just covered still apply. The main difference in this bottle to the last one is that this one is to have a footring

A tall bottle by Jim Malone (UK), 15 in/38 cm tall.
A slender and elegant bottle by Jim Malone. The black, rather austere tenmoku glaze serves to highlight the surety of the form.

underneath it. A footring means that I have to leave the base much thicker to allow for clay to be turned away at a later stage. This bottle would have a base thickness of at least one inch/2.5 cm.

In pulling up the wall I am beginning the rounded shape quite early. There is no real benefit here in making a straight cylinder.

Notice how the top is much narrower than the widest part of the pot. When making this type of pot it is essential that you 'throw' toward the middle of the wheel. You may find that you will need to 'collar' in a little after each pull to keep the diameter of the rim under control. I am continuing to form the rounded body of the bottle by gentle pushing from the inside and using my outside fingers as support. These roles are reversed as I come around the swelling where the outside fingers push gently inwards and the inside fingers act as support.

This bottle is to be squared in shape. Here, I have taken my finger and drawn it up the inside of the pot to form the basis of four corners. Later, when leatherhard, the pot will be beaten with a wooden paddle to emphasise its squareness. I have left the top open enough to get my hand inside. I have also used a rib to smooth the outside of the pot.

Collaring in the neck. First I collar in and then pull up a little, collar in, pull up. By alternating the movements I gradually narrow the opening and extend the clay upward. You may feel the need to lift the shoulder with a finger from the inside every so often.

Delicate finishing to the neck and lip. Keep a watchful eye on the scale of features like the rim of a bottle. In concentrating intently upon a particular feature like this, it is easy to lose sight of the scale and shape within the overall form of the pot.

Cutting away some of the surplus of clay from underneath. This is the initial stage of turning a footring.

Above
A squared bottle by the author. 11 in/28 cm tall.
A bottle made by the technique described on pages 64 and 65. I have decorated this piece by firstly brushing white slip onto each face and then drawing through the slip to reveal the body underneath. The ash glaze has then highlighted the drawn pattern in the way that only ash glaze can. The footring has been turned in the way I describe on page 98.

The bottle as it appears when I take it from the wheel. You can see where the footring will be and at the lefthand edge the corner of what will be a squared form. I leave it on the bat until the upper portion is dry enough to turn, the bottom will still be quite wet clay which I find the easiest and most responsive to turn. You can see the turning of this pot later in the book.

Chapter Eight
A Teapot

Every potter eventually wants to make a teapot. The teapot is arguably the ultimate challenge to the thrower; it combines three or four separately thrown elements that have to be combined to form a functional yet aesthetically pleasing whole.

The body of the pot needs to be fairly light in weight; a very heavy pot will test the strongest of wrists when it is full of tea. The lid, however you decide to sit it on your pot, should have some device that prevents it from falling off when the pot is tilted. The spout must pour properly without dribbling, and the handle has to be comfortable to grip and in physical and visual balance with the spout.

Historically, there have been many fine teapots for us to refer to and draw inspiration from. In China and Korea the ewer which was primarily intended for wine is the forerunner of the teapot and in Japan the cult of tea drinking has meant that there is a wealth of teapots both old and new. Hamada was a fine maker of teapots. In the West, and particularly in the UK, the teapot has a long and revered family line. English examples in cream ware or salt glaze from the 18th and early 19th centuries have much to offer us in terms of shape and orchestration. The popularity of tea as a drink and the challenge that the teapot has presented to the potter has meant that the teapot is to be found within the repertoire of most studio potters. I think that it is true that the teapot has, above all other pots, given the potter the most scope for the imaginative use of clay throughout its long and disparate history.

The teapot body, 2 lb. 4 oz.

I tend to like round, fat teapots. There is something about a teapot and all that it represents that seems to dictate to me, at least, that a full, generous shape is most appropriate. Below I have pulled up the wall as high as I wanted it and I am now beginning to swell out the rounded shape.

With the help of a throwing rib I am bending over the top $1\frac{1}{2}$ in. (4 cm) to form a flattened shoulder (overleaf). If the body requires more shaping, I can still get my fingers in. It really pays to have long, thin fingers!

I have formed the rim for the lid to sit on, by pushing down with the corner of the rib to leave a prominence standing proud. As I push down with the rib I have to support the shoulder of the pot with my finger on the inside. This type of lid seating is the simplest to form. Later, we will look at the making of a recessed ledge to take a drop-in lid which is a little more difficult to make.

Lastly, I can use the rib to smooth and flatten the shoulder which has the effect of sharpening the form and emphasising the point of change from body to shoulder.

Before I remove the pot from the wheel I need to ***carefully*** measure the opening so that I can make a well-fitting lid. As you can see in the photograph, the measurement that I take is a little less than the actual opening itself. A lid requires enough space for a small amount of movement. I use plastic callipers that are tightened fairly stiffly so there is little risk of them altering after I have set them.

The teapot lid, 8 oz

This teapot requires a lid that sits on top of the rim and is therefore exactly the same lid as I use for storejars and casseroles. The only difference is in its scale; the procedure is identical.

Centre the clay and form a shallow dish shape with a thick base and edge – a little like a doughnut.

Use your callipers to check that the diameter of the 'doughnut' is somewhere near the diameter that you will eventually require. At this stage it need only be an approximate measurement from the middle of the thick edge to the same point on the opposite edge.

Now comes the tricky bit! Take a chisel-ended tool, mine is an old heavy duty hacksaw with the teeth removed, and place the corner to the middle of the thick edge. Support the clay underneath with the fingers and steady the tool with the thumb. Gradually push the corner of the tool into the rim and downwards at the same time supporting all the time with the forefinger of the other hand.

Keep the tool steady. Push with one direct, but gradual movement and allow the shape of the tool to form the angle of the lid. Notice how the flange that is left standing is sloping inward so that it can guide your lid onto the pot.

I have smoothed and rounded all the edges with a soft sponge and here I am checking that the measurement is correct. It is this inner angle that is the important diameter as it is this point that fits into the opening on the pot. If the diameter is too small, I can ease the edge of the lid outwards with gentle pressure with one finger on the inside until, as in the photograph, this measurement is ***exactly*** what is recorded on the callipers. ***Lids that fit well are the result of careful and accurate measuring.***

Remove the lid from the bat and set it aside to firm up. If you are making more than one teapot it may well be worth recording for which pot this lid is intended.

Right
Two teapots by Jeff Oestreich (USA).
These two teapots were originally thrown on a potter's wheel and are wonderful examples of how the wheel can be used as a creative tool and does not limit the potter to round, symmetrical pots.
Each pot has been altered while still on the wheel much in the way that I have made the bottle square on page 64. Later they have been beaten and faceted to form sharp corners and angles. The bases have been added as strips of clay and then modelled and cut to suit.

The faceting and angular construction of these teapots imparts a solid, almost architectural quality. By removing the central axis of symmetry yet maintaining an essential physical balance the overall effect is to create pots with rhythm, movement and humour.
Photographs by Peter Lee.

Throwing the spout, 8 oz

There isn't a potter anywhere that enjoys throwing teapot spouts but we can't make a teapot without them, so here goes!

Centre the clay and open out without a base until you have formed a ring of clay with a thick wall.

Now 'collar' over to form a hollow 'volcano' shape. This movement takes a little practice but it is essential that you throw the spout as a cone from the very beginning.

The fingers begin the pull up right from the very bottom and the movement must always be inward to retain the cone shape.

After each pull upward the spout is collared in with the fingers squeezing gently and moving up the spout at the same time. Alternate between pulling up and collaring in. As you collar in, so the thickness of the wall increases a little to allow a further pull upward with one finger down inside the spout. As each pull finishes at the rim, you must clean away any slip and consolidate the clay by applying a little downward pressure. Spouts need to be thrown quite thinly and there is a tendency to split or tear at the end if they are allowed to become too wet or uneven.

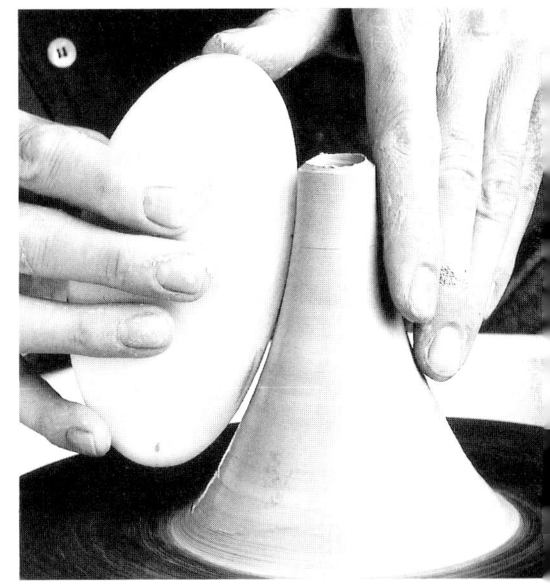

Finishing and smoothing the profile with a curved throwing rib.

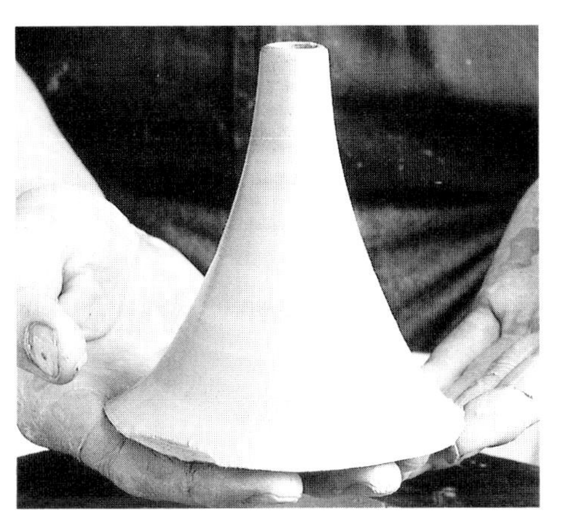

Remove the spout from the bat with a wire and place it carefully onto a wareboard to firm up.

We have now made all the individual parts. Set them aside until they have firmed enough to proceed. The body and the lid now have to be turned and the the teapot assembled.

I turn the base of the teapot in exactly the same way as I turned the base of the bottle on page 100. Notice once more how the thumb or forefinger of my left hand is steadying the end of the cutting tool. I can't repeat often enough how important this is.

The lid is set upon a small chuck that was thrown at the same time as the lid. I am turning away the clay at the top to form a shallow dome and a small step from the dome to the rim.

At the centre of the lid, score the clay with a pin and apply a ***small*** amount of slip. Push into place a small ball of soft clay and seal around the joint with the end of the finger.

Centre this small ball of clay and then shape it into a solid knob. If you want a hollow knob, then you will need to throw a small 'pot' and completely close over the top. Don't forget to drill a small hole from the back of the lid into the space within the knob to allow air to escape as the lid dries.

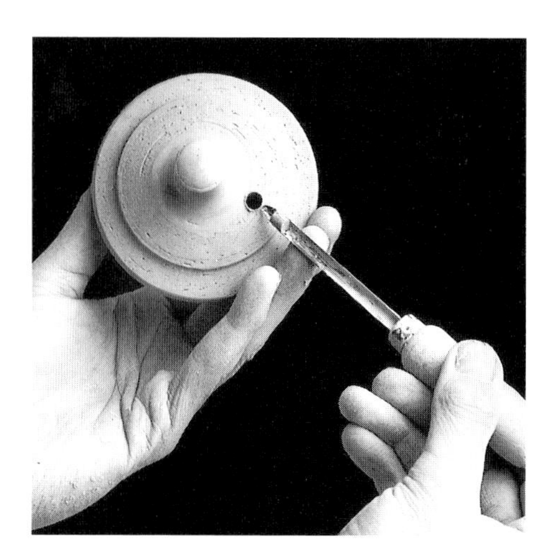

The lid will need a small hole to allow air in to the pot so that the tea can pour out. *Do not* try to clean the rough edges around this or any other detail until the clay has become bone dry.

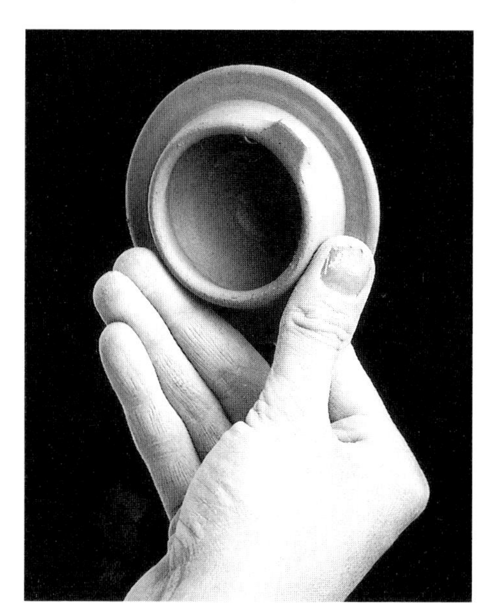

Underneath I always put a small 'catch' that hooks underneath the rim of the pot and helps prevent the lid falling off when the tea is being poured. To make this catch, a small piece of clay is stuck to the under rim and shaped with wet fingers.

Sticking on the spout

Before you start, make sure that you have a clear workspace, a bench whirler, a teapot hole borer, a knife, a soft sponge and a wire. Sit at your bench with some music playing in the background (it helps!) and begin by sticking the first spout firmly to the workbench.

Take your wire and with one, finely judged cut, draw it toward you as near to the correct angle as you can make it. Cutting off the spout from its base at the correct angle takes practice but if you can get it right first time, it saves an awful lot of time. Now, discard the unwanted base and dip the wider end of the spout in some water and leave it on the table until you are ready to use it.

The number and size of the holes that you drill into the pot will have a direct bearing on the way your pot will eventually pour. You must have as many as you can get within the space available so that a good pressure of tea will build up within the spout pushing it out as you pour.

To begin with, I lightly place the wetted end of the spout against the pot and then take it away again. The faint mark that is left behind is my guideline and the boundary of my holes.

I start with one line from top to bottom and then I fill in the gaps at each side until the whole space is filled. Clean up the rough edges of the holes inside the pot with a wooden modelling tool when the pot is ***bone dry***.

Score the clay around the outside of the holes and on the edge of the spout itself, and smear on a light coating of slip. Firmly press the spout into place and smooth the joint over, blending the clay into the body wall. ***Make sure that the end of the spout is at least as high as the rim of the pot itself otherwise your tea will pour out as you pour the water in***!

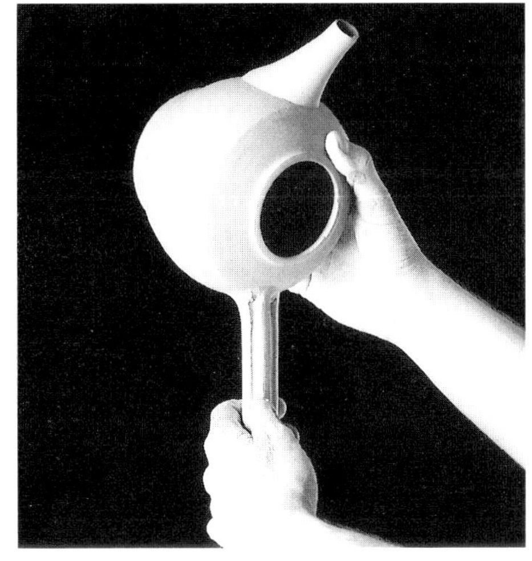

With the spout now firmly in place, a handle is applied in exactly the same way as for the jug on page 50. The handle requires that it should visually balance the spout. I have reshaped the handle by pushing it upwards. I feel that this new shape both complements the form of the pot and helps create a more harmonious whole.

The finished teapot with its lid in place.

A spout will usually need to be cut back at the very top to promote a better pouring lip. For me, it also improves the look of a spout. With the teapot directly in front of you at eye level take a sharp blade, I use a blade from a Stanley craft knife, and cut across from front to back. The spout will tend to 'unwind' clockwise during drying and firing. To counteract this phenomenon, the cut off must allow for some movement so make the cut 'left hand down' a little.

Make your cut in one, clean move and support the back edge with a finger to prevent it breaking.

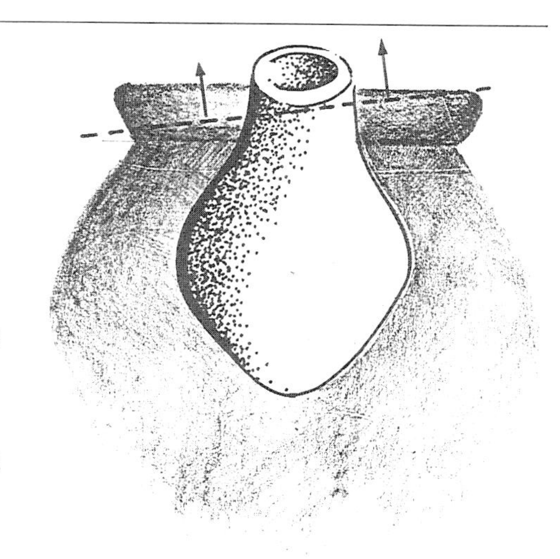

Right
Two salt-glazed teapots by the Author, 8 in/ 20.5 cm tall.
The upper teapot is very similar to the one that we have just made except that in this case I have textured the body of the pot with a pattern of lines.

In summary

1. *The teapot that I have shown you is just an example. It happens to be one that I make regularly but it is up to you to use these basic techniques to develop your own shapes and styles. Look around you at other teapots and try to absorb certain details that you like without actually copying one particular pot. I had no formal pottery training and learnt a great deal from inspecting other pots both old and new.*
2. *Be aware of the scale of your individual parts. It is difficult to begin with to make all the component parts so that when they fit together there is a uniformity of scale.*
3. *Keep your workspace clean and uncluttered.*
4. *When you come to join all the parts together, keep a towel near you so that you can regularly wipe your hands.*
5. *There is a lot to consider in making a teapot. Don't be discouraged if your first efforts are less than successful.*

The dotted line indicates the lowest level at which to cut off the spout. Any lower than this line and the tea would exit from the pot as it is filled without the need to tilt the pot. This detail is often overlooked in the beginners teapot but it is a mistake normally only made once!

Chapter Nine
Lids

If throwing a pot wasn't difficult enough there are a whole range of pots that require you to make a second piece before the pot can be called complete. The lid or cover is primarily a device to prevent dust or other foreign bodies from falling into the pot and to a certain extent keep the contents of the pot fresh or dry.

As with assembling a teapot, there are difficulties involved in matching the lid to the pot both physically and aesthetically and a certain amount of experience and practice is required to find a happy marriage.

There are a number of ways of covering a pot with a lid and the method that you choose will vary somewhat in

A selection of different lid types. Lids that sit in the pot or sit on the rim. Some with knobs, some with strap handles and some with neither. It's up to you to decide which configuration will suit your pot the best.

accordance with the type of pot that you are making. There are 'classic' combinations such as the 'ginger jar' and its cap-like cover but most other pots can carry whatever configuration of lid that you decide. The important point to remember is that the lid should work well within the overall function of the pot. For instance, a casserole lid should fit well and be easily and safely lifted when hot for instance, and that visually it should complete and enhance the entire form.

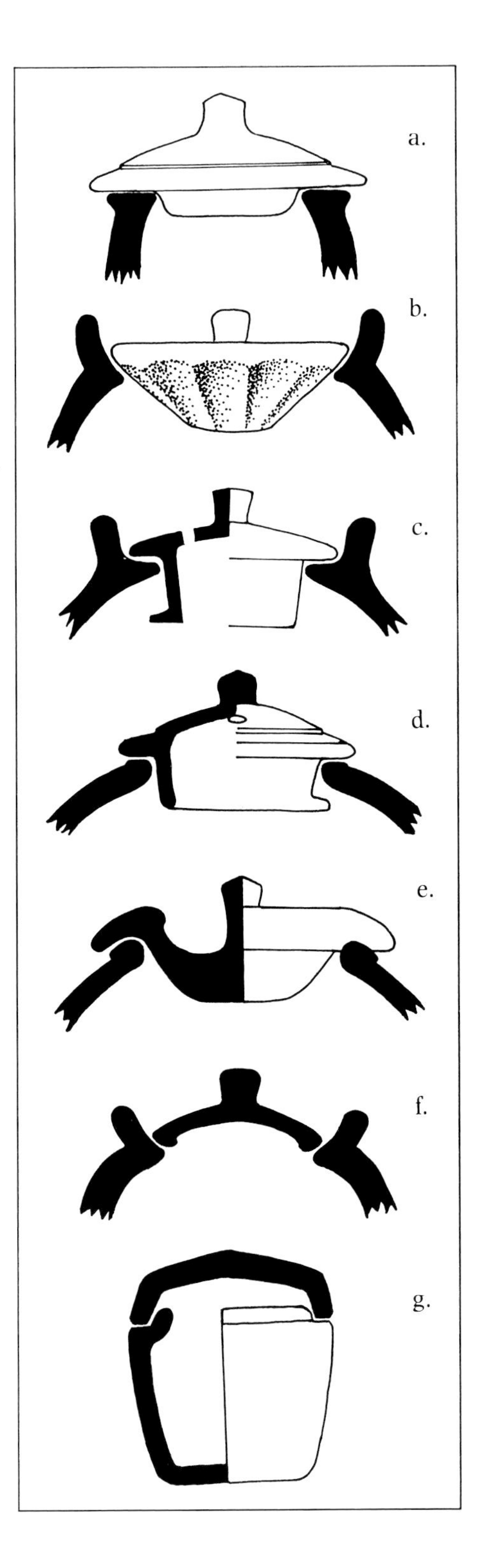

These are some of the most commonly used lid types. You will see that they either 'sit in' or 'sit on' the pot. The choice is yours but remember to consider the functional aspects before you decide.

a. A 'sit on' lid with a flange underneath to keep it in place. This is the same lid that I make on page 75.

b. A 'sit in' lid that I often use for teapots.

c. A 'sit in' lid that also has a flange underneath which helps prevent the lid from the tipping off when the pot is tilted. A small extension to the lower rim also helps in this respect by catching on the underneath of the ledge in the rim of the pot. You can get a better view of this in the photograph of a teapot lid on page 76.

d. A similar lid to (c) but this time sitting on the rim of the pot rather than in a gallery. See the teapot on page 79 for a photograph of this lid.

e. Another lid sitting on the rim of the pot. This time the lid is thrown the correct way up and the weight in the base of the lid helps keep it in place.

f. A domed lid that rests on an inner gallery. Usually very easily made by throwing 'off the hump' as a small saucer shape. The knob is thrown on after turning on a chuck.

g. Here, I have shown you a box and its lid although this lid and its seating are exactly the same as for the 'cap' of a ginger jar.

The lid of a large store jar by the Author, 12 in/ 31 cm diameter
This large lid shows in some detail the way in which it has been turned to complement the shape of the pot below it. With this particular kind of lid it is important that the outer edge is wider than the rim of the pot so that the lid overhangs a little. The lid will visually appear *not* to fit if this detail is overlooked even if the inner fitting is perfect.

In making the teapot we have already looked at the making of one kind of lid. The very same lid, but much bigger, can be used for a store jar or a casserole, indeed any pot where the lid sits on a flat rim. I use this type of lid more than any other. The benefit to the thrower of this kind of lid arrangement is that the seating for the lid is relatively simple to make.

I measure the opening of a store jar with the callipers, leaving an allowance of a couple of millimetres each side so that the lid will retain some movement.

I have centred the clay and opened it out to form a small dish shape with a thick edge. Be generous with the thickness through the base also.

The measurement need only be approximate at this stage but be sure that your thick edge is near to the calliper setting.

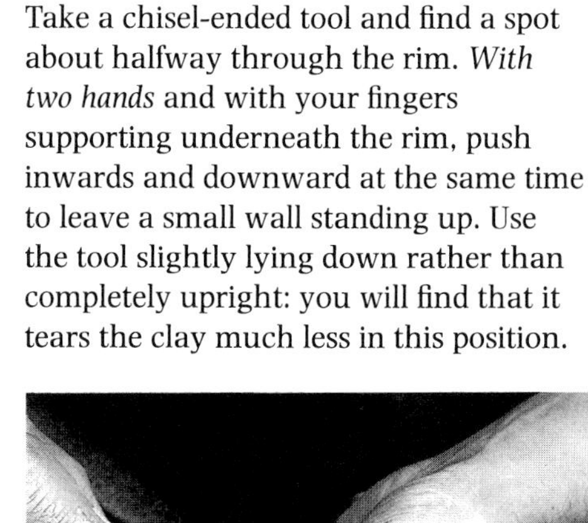

Take a chisel-ended tool and find a spot about halfway through the rim. *With two hands* and with your fingers supporting underneath the rim, push inwards and downward at the same time to leave a small wall standing up. Use the tool slightly lying down rather than completely upright: you will find that it tears the clay much less in this position.

Since the last picture I have rounded and smoothed both edges with my fingers and a soft, wet sponge. Be careful not to overdo this as the action of the sponge will take away the surface clay and leave any sand or grog standing as a rough surface. You may find that the soft strip of leather that we used earlier will provide a better finish once the edges are round.

I am checking that the measurement is completely accurate. If it isn't, then minor adjustment can be made by carefully and gradually pushing outward with a finger on the inside, just below the rim.

The lid can be cut from the bat immediately and set aside to firm up enough for turning. We have already looked at the turning of a lid of this type on page 75.

Another widely used lid is the 'drop in' type which is much easier to make although the seating on the pot is more complicated than the flat rim we have just looked at.

Firstly, the seating for the lid. I have thrown a pot with a thick, rounded rim. To make the 'gallery', I use a wooden tool with a spoon-like rounded back. Other potters simply use their finger. The tool is used to split the thick rim by pushing down on the inner edge while at the same time supporting the rim on the outside with the forefinger of the left hand. The danger here is that you will exert too much pressure on the entire rim and badly distort the pot. This is not an easy manoeuvre and requires practice.

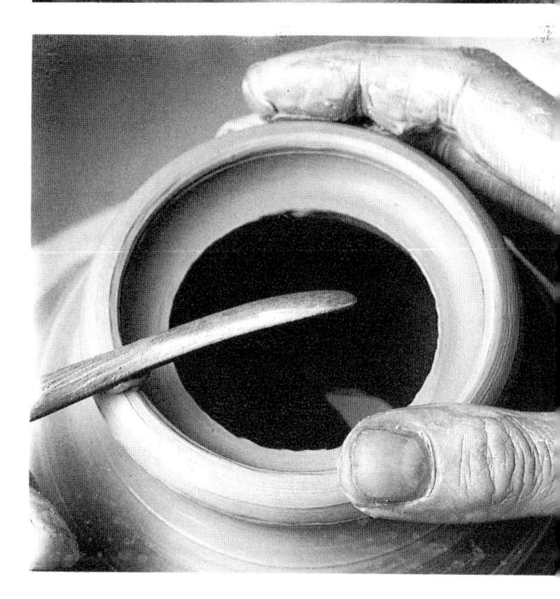

Here, I am using the natural roundness of the pad of my forefinger to shape the contour of the gallery. The rim is rounded with the strip of leather and the inner ledge smoothed with a soft sponge.

The lid that fits into this type of seating is thrown 'off the hump' as we call it. That is to say, a large lump of clay is centred on the wheel and the lids are thrown by using only the correct amount of clay at the top of the centred piece. Each time you want to begin a new lid a portion of the 'hump' is sectioned off and the lid made from this. As each one is finished, it is wired off and lifted away ready to begin another one. This saves you the problem of weighing out a number of small pieces of clay and having to centre each one individually.

Throwing 'off the hump' is a useful method of making a range of smaller items. Small bowls, teacups, teapot spouts as well as lids can be made this way. I find it particularly useful for quickly making a large number of small bowls to use as glaze tests. Here I have sectioned off enough clay to make a 'drop in' lid.

Pinch and pull out the clay between thumb and forefinger to create a flange but leave the centre portion standing. This will be the knob. Think of the lid as an almost flat saucer shape with a knob in the middle.

Measure across the lid to check that you have the correct diameter. Notice how, for this lid, I have altered the callipers to the crossed position because the measurement on the pot is between two inner points rather than across a flat rim.

Cut a deep 'V' shape underneath the lid with a pointed cutting tool. Notice how the weight of this type of lid is in its base which helps to keep the lid sitting in the pot.

With the wheel revolving very slowly, place a wire into the 'V' and allow the wheel to make one revolution so that the wire loops around. Now pull the wire toward you and the loop will tighten and slice off the lid. Make sure that you keep the wire level. Lift the lid from the hump onto a wareboard to dry and begin your next lid by sectioning off as before.

The 'drop in' lid requires very little or no turning if you have been neat in undercutting the 'V' during the throwing. However, just to be different I use a sharp knife to pare away eight segments from the back of the lid to give me a 'petal' finish. I find this quicker than having to re-centre the lid to turn it and it makes for a slightly more individual finish.

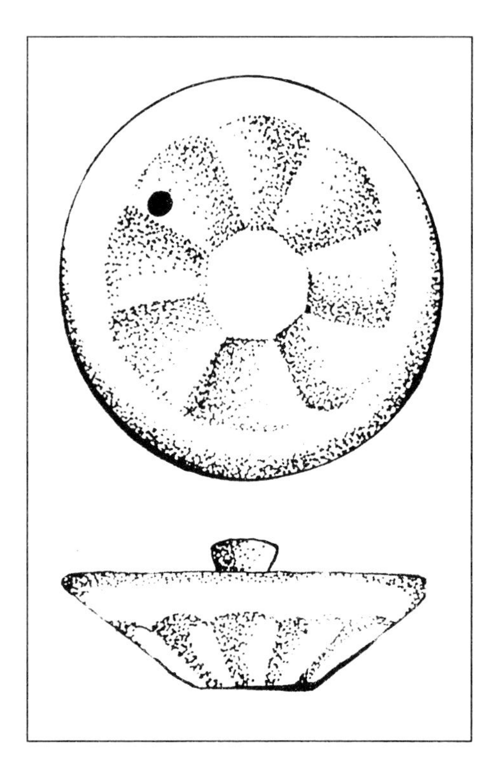

A 'drop in' teapot lid showing the knife cuts on the back.

Applying a strap handle

All the time you are making a pot, you should also be making decisions about the form and orchestration of what you are doing. Decisions, for instance, about the height in relation to the width or whether this particular pot would function better with a 'sit on' or a 'sit in' lid? Is a footring called for or should it be flat based? etc. etc.

There are decisions to make concerning the features of your lid and one of them is how will you be able to pick it up? A lid will often need a means of lifting it up, especially if its diameter is wider than the average hand grip or if visually the pot requires it. We have already seen how to 'throw' on a knob to a lid when we looked at the teapot lid. One other popular option is the strap handle.

The handle itself is made in exactly the same way as the handle that we made for the jug on pages 48 and 49. A length or strip of handle is pulled from a lump and laid down on a ***clean*** workbench. The cross section that you choose is entirely up to you. I have made a 'U' shaped handle by pulling my thumb down the centre. More important is the scale or weight of your handle. It is a common mistake in the early stages to make additions to a pot that are completely out of scale. Try not to lose sight of the scale of the handle in relation to the lid and to the pot in your focussed attempts to pull it and then attach it.

I have turned the top of my lid and immediately placed it onto a bench whirler. At this stage the lid needs to be a soft to medium leatherhard. If it has become too dry your handle runs the risk of cracking at the joint.

Score the two areas that will receive

the handle and add a ***small*** amount of thick slip or slurry.

Cut a section of your handle from the strip with a clean potter's knife. You will find that the length you will need to make the arched handle will be much less than you initially think. Here, I have placed it into position and am now lightly pressing down the ends ready to be 'thumbed' down.

Having put the handle exactly where I want it to be, I thumb off the corners trying to keep the same angle on each movement. The last move is a rounded 'wipe' of the thumb to form a 'sweep' at the two ends.

All that remains is to gently refine the 'line' or arch of the handle and to ***lightly*** sponge the edges. In particularly dry weather when pots are prone to dry very quickly, I will turn this lid upside down onto the damp pot so that the handle dries gradually inside.

In summary

1. *Take extra special care in measuring for your lids. A lid will only fit properly if you measure accurately.*
2. *Use the same clay for your lid as that which you used for making the pot.*
3. *Pay particular attention to the finish or neatness of the edges of your lids.*
4. *Be mindful of the relative scale of your handle to the lid and pot.*

A burnished earthenware bowl by Duncan Ross (UK), $8\frac{1}{4}$ in/21 cm tall.

Depending on the type and style of pots that you make, various pottery making techniques can be used to achieve very different finishes. Duncan Ross has produced a smooth, pristine surface to accept his precise, graphic decoration by turning and smoothing the outside of the leatherhard pot with the use of cutting tools and throwing ribs. The overall effect is quite magnificent.

This kind of finish is totally appropriate, indeed essential for this pot. However, my style of pottery, my glazes, in fact my whole personality requires a different approach as you will see. It is this search for a personal vocabulary in pottery that is so very difficult to find and there are many very adequate throwers who never quite find it.

Chapter Ten
Turning

For some strange, unrecorded reason 'turning' in pottery has sometimes been looked upon by many potters as something of a chore. How many times have I heard a production potter boast, 'I don't turn anything, it's a waste of time'. What nonsense! Turning is as much a part of the creative process of throwing as the initial forming itself. The dull, rather over-engineered turning that we often see underneath some poor quality pottery is more a reflection of that potter's lack of understanding of how turning or trimming should be carried out rather than any unresponsive quality in the process itself.

Having said all that, I firmly believe that any pot that doesn't require turning as part of its overall shape and concept should be left alone. I would *never* encourage a student to turn the base of a flat mug or jug. A neat, clean wire pattern is a far more suitable finish. Neither would I like to see a potter trimming down the outside of a thrown pot in the vain hope that by doing so it will somehow improve. Nothing kills the freshness or spontaneity of a thrown form more than the paring down of the profile to correct a badly thrown shape or to reduce the weight of a thickly thrown wall. If a pot requires this kind of remedial treatment throw it away and make a better one.

Try to think of turning as an integral part of the making process and not as an afterthought. If you watch a Japanese potter look at a bowl, the first thing that he will do is turn it over and inspect the turned footring. Here, he will tell you, is the potter's true character. Nothing is hidden. Often unglazed, the quality of the cutting is an open book to the trained eye and can reveal much about a potter's understanding of, and attitudes to, pot making.

I have seen a short film of Hamada turning a footring onto a bowl. In two minutes, he gives a lesson in correct turning that every potter should see. The bowl is recentred onto a 'chuck' and with a loop of metal strip he cuts away the clay in thick swathes. The foot appears after two or three movements just as though he knew that it was there and that all he had to do was to reveal it. A couple of taps to the underneath tells him that the thickness is right and the bowl is lifted from the wheel. The marks that the cutting edge left behind are all part of the feeling that this bowl was made by hand and totally appropriate in this context.

Of course I understand that not all potters want to produce pots that contain this type of hewn quality to the turning. Duncan Ross's bowl on page 90 is an example of a surface that needs to be flat and smooth to accommodate the decoration. There are many styles of pot making that call for a more controlled and deliberate style of turning. However, my message is: Turn your pots as though you mean it. If you find, as I did, that you come to enjoy the turning of your pots then turn them with energy and confidence and not as though you would really rather be doing something else.

A bowl with combed decoration and ash glaze by the Author, $4\frac{1}{2}$ in/11.5 cm tall.
This rounded bowl has been turned because I needed to create a footring from the thickness of clay deliberately left in the base. You can clearly see the marks left by the turning tool, highlighted by the glaze, as diagonal lines travelling down the bowl. After turning, the bowl was dipped in a white slip and the combed marks were made with a serrated plastic tool.

When to turn

A pot will need to 'firm up' a little before it can be turned. How firm you allow the pot to become is, to a great extent, up to you. Leatherhard is a term that is often used to describe clay that is ready to turn although there is no specific meaning to exactly what 'leatherhard' means. For instance, I like to turn clay when it is very soft, almost as soft as when I threw the pot. I find that only when the clay is this soft do I achieve the kind of quality to the cutting that I really want. Other potters would find this method totally unworkable. They need their pots to have dried a little more, in other words to have become soft leatherhard or 'cheese hard'. Clay which has dried even further can be 'hard leatherhard' and has the firmness of a bar of soap. So, firmness is a little like the proverbial piece of string and is therefore a matter of personal preference.

It is a fact though, that the softer the clay is when you turn your pots, the easier you will find it and the kinder it will be to the cutting edge of your tools. If turning becomes a real struggle, if the clay falls from your pot as crumbs rather than strips, if the cutting edge leaves behind the small but regular bounce marks that we call chatter marks, if your fingers and wrists begin to ache or if the clay has begun to change to a lighter colour then you will know that your pot has become too dry.

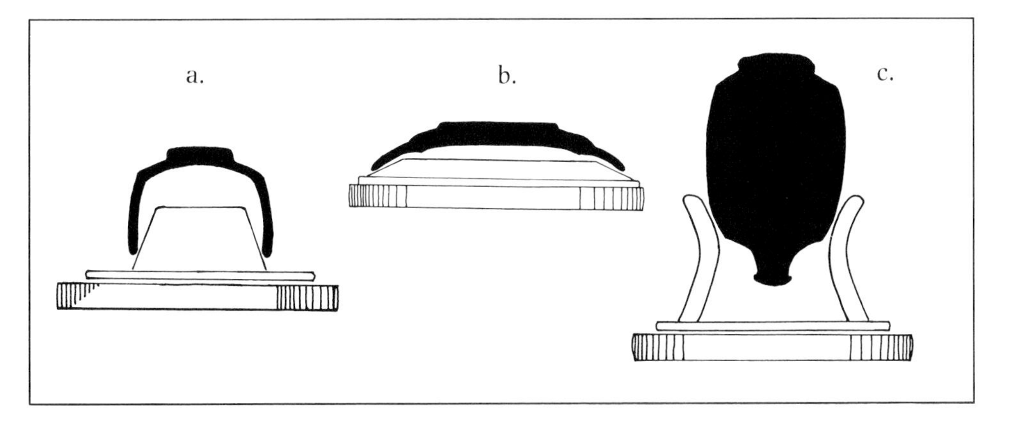

a. A small bowl resting on a chuck the shape of which is designed to provide a snug fit. If this chuck were any flatter then the bowl may not sit firmly during turning, any taller and the bowl may get stuck or the rim may split.

b. A plate rests on its rim on a broad chuck.

c. A bottle form sitting in a tall hollow chuck. This type of chuck can be used for any shape that will not fit over a solid chuck. However, this kind of chuck should not be used to turn a 'better' shape as a correction to bad throwing.

Re-centring

To be able to turn your pot, it will need to be put back onto the potter's wheel exactly in the centre and usually upside down. There are a number of ways of doing this but by far the easiest and most efficient way is to use what we call a 'chuck'.

Broadly speaking a chuck is a simple means of supporting and centring a pot that also has the benefit of preventing any damage to the rim. As you can see in the diagrams above, a chuck (normally made from clay) can be solid in order to take a bowl or a plate. Alternatively, it can be a hollow shape to accommodate the neck of a bottle.

Throw your chuck ***on a bat***

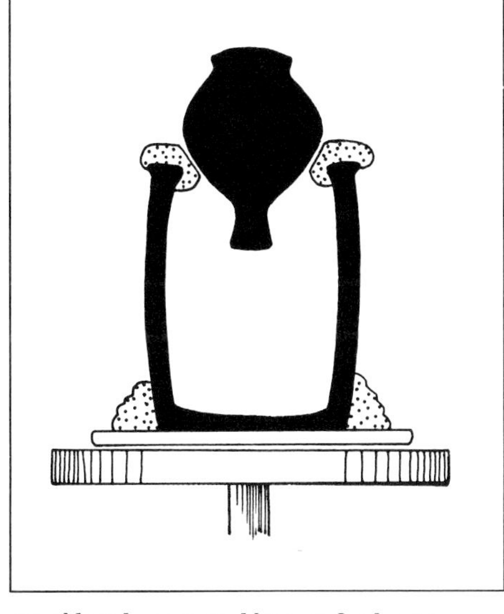

An old and unwanted biscuit-fired pot is centred on the wheel and anchored down with clay. A coil of clay is fixed to the rim and cut circular inside with a knife or a needle held steadily while the pot is rotated. The pot to be turned can now be placed onto the soft clay without fear of damage.

Whichever way you choose, you should always use a chuck whenever possible. The use of lumps of clay to anchor a pot to the wheel is bad practice as is wetting the rim and relying on suction. These methods will lead to damaged rims that can never be repaired to that same standard of freshness of line. Often the difference between a good and a bad pot is nothing more than a professional attitude in the making.

immediately after you have finished throwing your pots so that they can 'firm up' together. They will need to have roughly the same moisture content for the chuck to work properly. As an easier and, I think, quicker alternative to the larger, hollow chucks, I often use an old, biscuit-fired pot with a wide neck as a chuck. This I centre on the wheel and then firmly anchor down with clay. Around the rim I place a coil of clay that will receive the pot that is to be turned. Because the coil is soft, there is no damage to the leatherhard pot.

Turning a small bowl

I have 'thrown' this chuck into a bat at the same time that I threw the bowl. I have repositioned the bat on the wheel so that the chuck is centred and anchored it firmly to a pad of clay as I showed you earlier. Here, I am trimming the edge of the chuck to the correct size so that the rim of the bowl comes approximately halfway down the side and makes a snug, 'gripping' fit.

I have set the bowl onto the chuck. The chuck, if it is properly centred, will help you to centre the bowl. Providing the bowl is level as it turns, it should be centred. Minor alterations can be made by easing the bowl over to one side or the other. As you can see, I tend to prefer the looped type of turning tool rather than those which are strips of metal that bend at right angles at the end. I simply find that the loop cuts through the clay more cleanly. This preference is purely personal and there is nothing wrong with the other type if you find them more suitable.

Notice again how the hands are linked to give me a steady grip on the tool and to prevent the tool from wandering across the surface of the clay.

Work on the outside profile first and get that right before going on to the underneath. If you make the inner well too large too soon then you will not be able to reduce the outer profile enough if you need to.

A bowl by the Author, 6 in/15.5 cm diameter. After turning, this bowl was covered with a thick white slip which was textured with upward strokes from a coarse brush. The 'plant' drawing was then made through the slip with the point of a knife.

See how much clay I am removing with one cutting movement. In fact, I try to make the inner well with one and no more than two cutting movements. I can do this because the clay is soft and because I am confident that I know how much thickness of clay there is for me to cut away without having to worry about going through. Use the thumb on the end of the turning tool for steadiness.

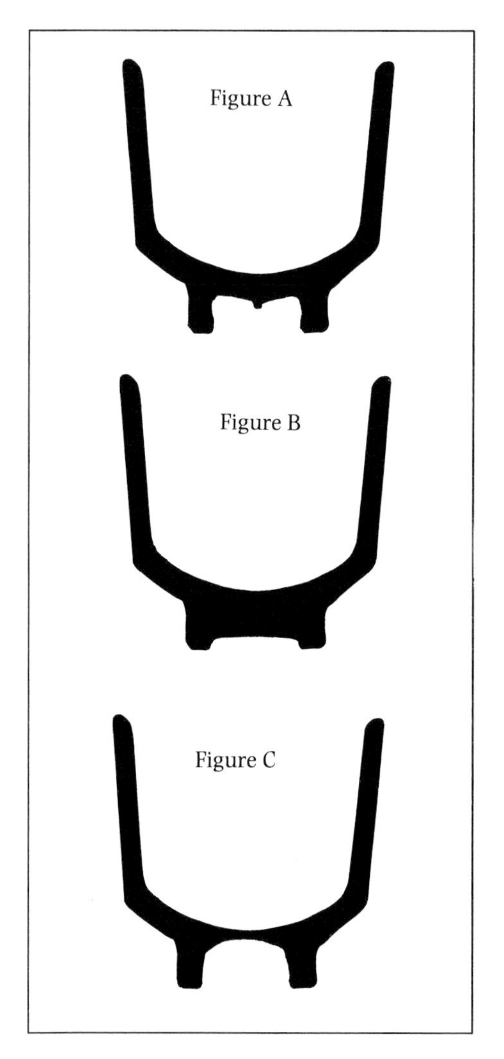

The underneath or inner space of a turned footring should follow the curve or direction of the wall of the pot. Figure A shows a correct profile. The line of the bowl as it comes around to the footring is continued underneath and carries on through to the other side. In Figures B and C the level underneath is offensive to the eye and the differences in thicknesses of clay may cause your pot to crack as it dries. In Figure B not enough clay has been taken away which leaves the base too thick and in Figure C too much which leaves the base very thin, the wall uneven and a nasty surprise to the eye when the pot is turned over.

The turning is almost complete and I am putting a small bevel onto the outside and inside edges of the foot. Notice how clean everything is. Hands, bat and cutting tool are free of slip or clay crumbs.

The finished bowl. Try to aim to turn a bowl of this scale in no more than a minute. Turning quickly and boldly minimises the amount of fussing and fiddling that you can do and will ultimately help you to produce fresh, spontaneous turning.

The shape of the footring can have a tremendous effect upon the character of a bowl. Bowls that are basically the same shape can alter dramatically depending on whether a footring is wider or narrower at the point at which it touches the surface on which it stands (see diagrams).

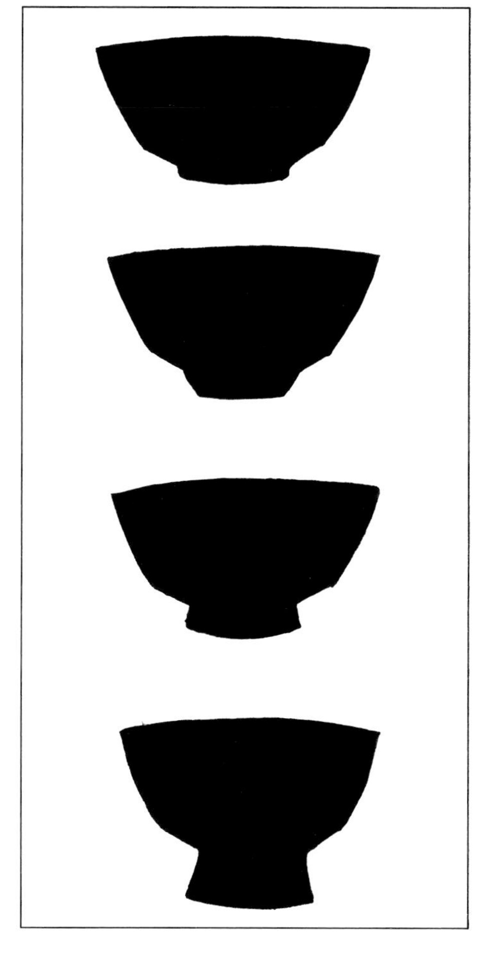

These four bowls are exactly the same except for the shape of the footring. See how the character of each is altered dramatically by the choice of foot. A useful exercise is to make a number of identical bowls and then to turn different footrings onto them and decide for yourself which have 'worked' the best in terms of complete form.

Turning a plate

This is the plate that we made earlier in the book. You can see straight away that the chuck is much wider this time to allow for the wider rim. The plate sits quite securely on the chuck; in fact, the wider the form the less there is any tendency for it to slip off.

All of the rules that we have talked about in turning the bowl apply here.

1. Hands are linked. ***Very important.***
2. Outside profile is dealt with first.
3. Soft clay makes cutting effortless.

Almost finished. I am just putting the finishing touches to the edges of the footring itself. The small button in the middle of the well is largely aesthetic. It is often seen on pots from the Far East where I believe it acted as a form of insurance in that it prevented the plate from sagging during firing.

Notice how I have 'turned' a step into the outer wall of the plate. This will coincide with that point on the inside where the well becomes the rim. Hopefully this step will attract a pooling of the glaze during the firing and become a decorative feature. I also believe that a step of this kind physically strengthens the form preventing warping later during the drying and firing.

Turning a bottle

As you can see I have turned the bottle upside down into the chuck where it rests neatly on its shoulder. Ideally the chuck will be slightly softer than the bottle so that damage doesn't occur. The diagram on page 93 shows you exactly how this works. Make sure that the pot is level as it revolves and you are ready to begin cutting.

Remember turn quickly and boldly. Try to get into the habit of 'attacking' your turning rather than spending too long taking away far too little clay over a long period. I would envisage that a pot of this type would take no longer than $1\frac{1}{2}$ minutes from the time I start cutting to finishing. Sit comfortably or stand with your body close to the wheel, don't try to turn at arms length.

Right *A squared and salt-glazed bottle by the Author, 13 in/33 cm tall.*
This bottle is very similar to the one that we have made in this book. You can see quite clearly how, by gently beating the sides, I have made the corners sharp and given definition to the shoulder. Notice how the line of ascent from the footring into the body of the bottle gives the whole pot a visual lift. The wrong line here and the pot will look as though it has sagged.

Hold the tool close to its end. The thumb of your other hand provides a steady grip. Cut away plenty at a time.

The finished footring. You can see that I have cut a spiral pattern into the base simply by allowing the tool to cut quickly through the soft clay. This is not a contrived and very deliberate mark but the natural impression of the tool as it moves quickly from the centre to the outer edge. The cutting tool has also begun to emphasise the squareness by cutting across the corner to create a kind of scalloped effect.

Later, as the pot firms up a little, I will beat the sides with a wooden paddle to 'square' it even more and to sharpen the corners. You can see the overall effect in the photograph on page 127.

In summary

1. *As soon as a bowl or plate is firm enough to support its own weight, turn it over and allow it to dry on its rim. After turning, do the same thing until the bowl is bone dry and ready for the kiln. Hopefully, by doing this, you will prevent the rim from warping and as a bonus you will be drying the piece more evenly thereby cutting down the risk of cracking due to shrinkage stresses.*
2. *Try to turn while the clay is still soft.*
3. *Unless it is a practical impossibility because of excessive size, always use a chuck to hold your pot firmly while turning.*
4. *Remove the clay from the outside profile of a footring before dealing with the inner well.*
5. *Turn your pots with confidence and conviction.*
6. **Remember** *you are not trying to make pots that look as though they were made in a factory on a machine. Your pots* ***should*** *retain the echoes of their making, the marks of the tool, the slight variance of line that come from a casual but controlled hand. Don't overwork your pots. A turned pot should not look as though it has been machined. Allow the clay to speak. Try not to fuss and fiddle with your pots; you will only succeed in robbing them of their character.*
7. *I will say it again.* **Look, look, look** *at lots of other pots both contemporary and historical. See how they are turned and initially imitate the ones that really attract your attention.*

Chapter Eleven
Faceting a Small Bowl

Quite a number of my pots are cut sided or 'faceted'. Since seeing some faceted Korean pots many years ago, I have felt an affinity with this kind of decoration and it is certainly a technique that attracts a lot of interest whenever I have demonstrated it. It is a way of decorating pots that is part of the 'bones' of the pot and requires no further decorative treatment unless you particularly desire it. The lines that the cuts create often provide the covering glaze with an opportunity to 'break' to a different colour thus highlighting the decoration. My glazes are often made with wood ash and are particularly suited to this type of structural decoration as is salt glazing which seeks out and emphasises any mark or edge on a pot.

Faceting need not be restricted to small pots like the one that I am going to show you. Much larger pots can be made by making the cuts at a later stage (see Jim Malone's bottle on page 63 for instance). I make a lot of bottles which are thrown in one piece and then faceted later just prior to turning, once the clay has firmed up a little.

A Korean honey jar, probably 19th century, 10 in/25.5 cm high.
It was the faceting on many of the Korean pots that first influenced Hamada and Bernard Leach into faceting many of their own pots. Since then the technique has become popular amongst potters as a decorative effect. The running, dark, treacle-coloured glaze on this particular jar has flowed to heighten the effect of the cut lines. This actual pot belonged to Bernard Leach and is now part of the collection at the Crafts Study Centre in Bath, UK.
Photograph courtesy of the Holburne Museum Crafts Study Centre.

Faceted Yunomi or teacup 1 lb. 4 oz.

The faceted *Yunomi* that we are going to make is faceted during the throwing and then shaped from the inside. With practice, this technique can be used for other, more complicated pots such as teapots. (You may like to refer to *Ceramic Review*, Number 108, 1987.)

Pots which are to be faceted have to be thrown almost twice as thick as you would normally make them to allow for the cuts to be made. Here, I have thrown a cylinder with a thick base and I have

smoothed the outside of the pot with a straight-sided rib. It is extremely important that the walls of the cylinder be perfectly smooth because the faceting tool* has a roller which follows the contours of the wall.

*The faceting tool is in fact a cheese slicer which can be found in kitchen shops. You can see it clearly in the photograph on page 14 in the bottom righthand corner.

Left
Examples of other faceted pots taken from my sketchbooks. Some of these pots can be made in the same way as the bowl we are about to see i.e. faceted at the time of throwing. Other, larger pots can be thrown and faceted later after they have stiffened a little and just prior to turning. With these pots I suggest you begin your cut at the ***top*** of the pot and work downwards to the base. ***Remember*** that you don't have to facet ***any*** pot during throwing if you find this difficult. All pots can be cut after they have firmed up a little but you must remember to throw the pot with a thicker wall and with the correct shape.

Each cut is made with a firm, easy movement from the bottom to the top. ***Keep the roller against the wall of the pot throughout the entire movement.*** The tendency, in early attempts, is to move away from the pot as the hand reaches the top. You must avoid this. A finger pressed lightly against the inside rim helps to prevent the rim from depressing inward.

I make the first cut and then find the opposite point on the rim to make the second. Carry on in that fashion, cutting opposite facets, until the whole pot is completed.

Now, with the hands connected for steadiness, gently push out the shape of the bowl from the inside. Keep your eyes on the profile all the time and be careful not to push out more than you need as you will not be able to push it back again from the outside. The wheel needs to be revolving at a slow to medium speed at this point. Too slow and you will find fingermarks coming through, too fast and it will be very difficult to control the form.

The finished bowl. See how the cut lines follow the form of the bowl. All that remains for this bowl is to be turned on a chuck as we did on page 94.

In summary

1. *Always cut from bottom to top when faceting during the throwing with very wet clay. Keep the roller or guide bar against the wall of the pot all the way up the cut.*
2. *Cut firmly and decisively.*
3. *Shape from the inside using as much finger contact as possible. You may even find that a small, soft sponge is a better method.*
4. *This particular pot looks complicated. It really is much easier than you think.*

Left
Small faceted teabowl or Chawan by the author, 5 in/12.5 cm diam.
This little bowl was made in exactly the way I have just shown you except that I have drawn the facet cutter across the bowl at an angle rather than from bottom to top in a straight line. Notice how, that by turning the footring, the bottom edge of each facet has been cut neatly and also faintly scalloped. The line or angle of growth from the footring up into the bowl is very important. It is this line that can often determine whether your bowl has visual lightness. A badly conceived line, perhaps a bulging profile or one that meanders, can make your bowl appear heavy or slumped.

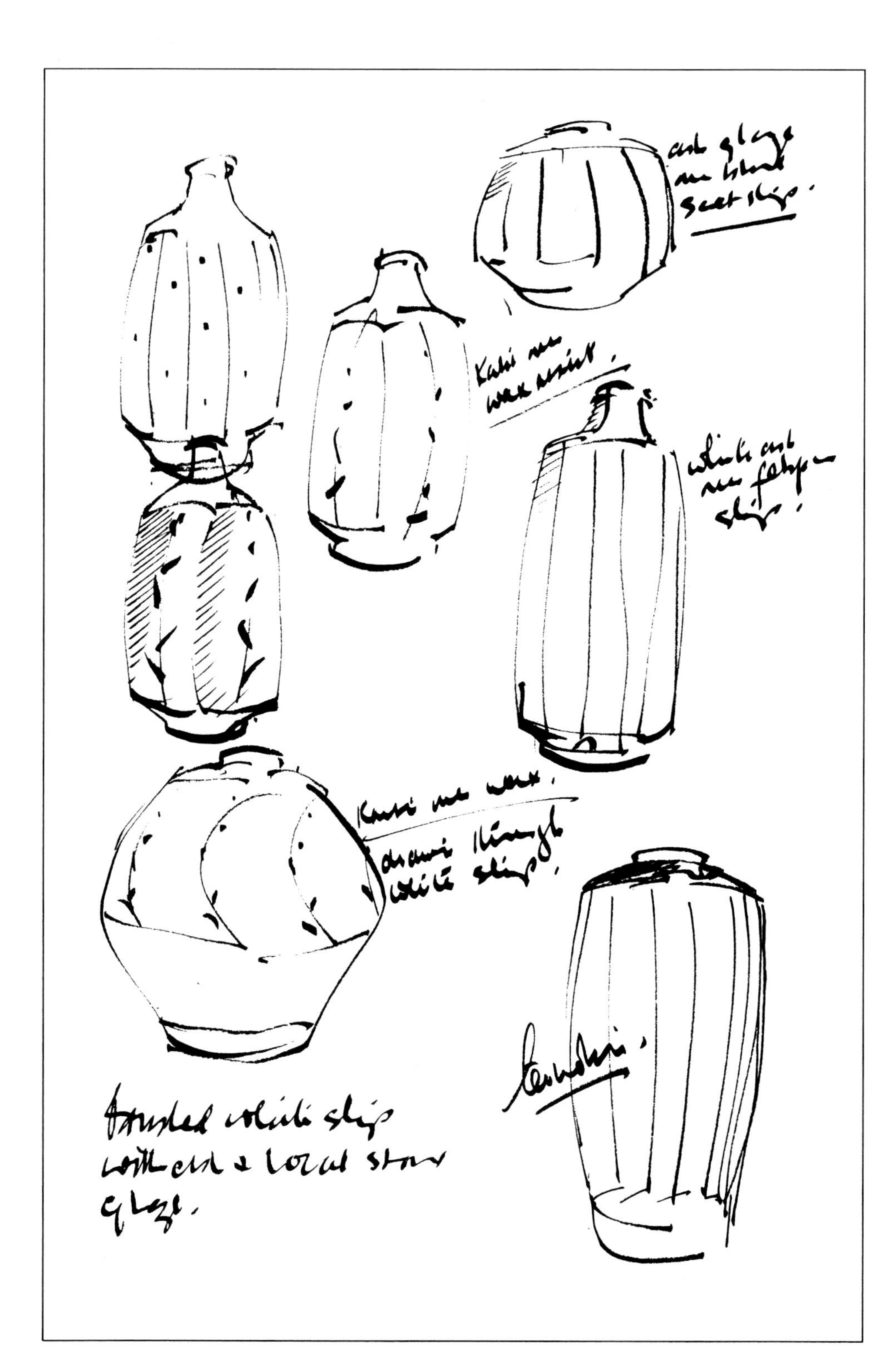

Chapter Twelve
Design

I firmly believe that to acquire the skills to throw a lump of soft clay into a cylindrical form or bowl shape is only half the battle in making a 'good' pot. The other half is knowing what to do with those skills. I have seen a great many very adequate throwers who made very poor pots simply because they hadn't taken the trouble to look at and get a feel for hand-thrown pottery. It saddens me terribly to hear people who 'play' at being potters deriding an excellent pot because of its 'roughness' in the turning or asymmetrical rim simply because they haven't taken the time and trouble to look further than their own kitchens in their search for what constitutes excellence in a thrown pot.

Many people come to pottery with very little experience of hand-thrown pots. Evening classes in pottery are very popular and often difficult to get into and yet it is often the case that students, while wishing to work with clay, have had very little contact with good quality handmade pots.

Handmade pottery has a whole new and very different set of standards that have to be understood. There is little point in making handmade pots that poorly imitate industrially-made wares. Yet so often I see students measuring their efforts against an industrial standard. I see pots that have been thrown too lightly, rims that are thin and brittle, excessive turning that has robbed the pot of all its character and life. Throwing has a language all of its own; a pot can be read like a book and the story that it tells should be about the materials from which it is made and the character of the potter that made it. Your pots should quickly become a part of yourself and to that end, it is vital that you begin to understand and respect the traditions and conventions of handthrown pottery.

I am not trying to say that all pottery **must** be traditional in its feel. Far from it. There is as much room in ceramics for individuality and personal style as there are potters who want to make pots. The message that I am trying to convey is simply this: Pottery can be, and should be, great fun but it is also a serious subject worthy of the greatest respect. If you are serious about learning to throw good pots (you bought this book!) then do some homework. Look at the best quality pots wherever and whenever you can find them in museums or craft galleries. Find some books, buy a few pots, make drawings. Isolate those pots from history that really attract your attention and use their best qualities in your own pots.

Immerse yourself in the subject so that as you come to make your own pots you will have a foundation of visual experience that will help you to understand and answer the questions of form and function that you will be posed as you sit at the wheel.

Left
This is a typical page from one of my own sketchbooks. Use a sketchbook to record new ideas and to clarify a shape or detail in your own mind before you start work.

A small lidded bowl or box by Bernard Leach, 4 in/10 cm high.

Bernard Leach was the founding father of the modern studio pottery movement. In a long potting career he tried his hand at almost all the different areas of making pottery. He made pots in stoneware, earthenware, raku, porcelain and salt glaze using many different methods of decoration, yet his own distinctive and personal style always shone through.

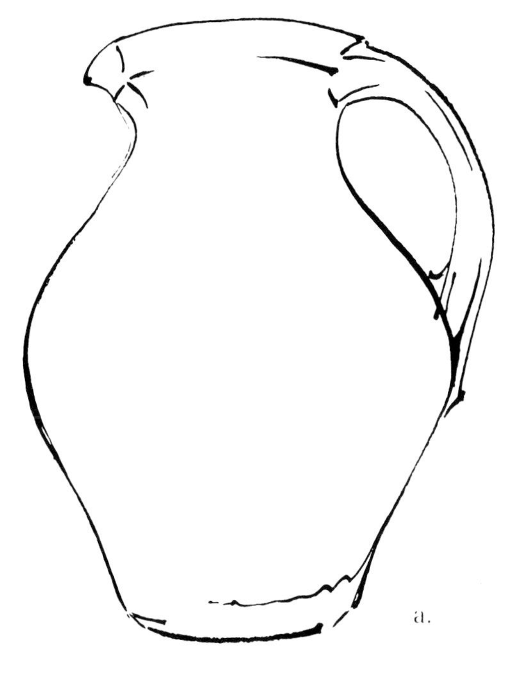
a.

I want to use this drawing of a jug to illustrate some of the questions that you must ask yourself when making a pot. *I am not putting forward this particular jug as the only correct solution to a jug form.* In fact, this is a very traditional pitcher shape that has been made tens of thousands of times. Indeed, there are many, many jug forms which can be every bit as successful as this one but equally there are many ways of getting it wrong. These few basic guidelines will, I hope, help you to see your way through the maze although any diagrammatical analysis must eventually give way to an intuitive grasp of form.

1. The handle starts and finishes on a prominence. There is a double rim that provides a horizontal line that serves to lead the eye from the jug into the handle. The fattest part of the belly is a natural point for the handle to terminate.

2. A natural and flowing curve to the handle creates a shape between its inner edge and the neck of the jug. This rounded inner space is accentuated by adding clay in the gap between handle and jug to form a rounded and natural looking lower joint. The amount of curve in the handle determines the distance between itself and the jug. Generally, the taller and more slender the pot, the closer the handle will be to the pot. An excessively rounded handle, even on a rounded jug, can look disproportionately large.

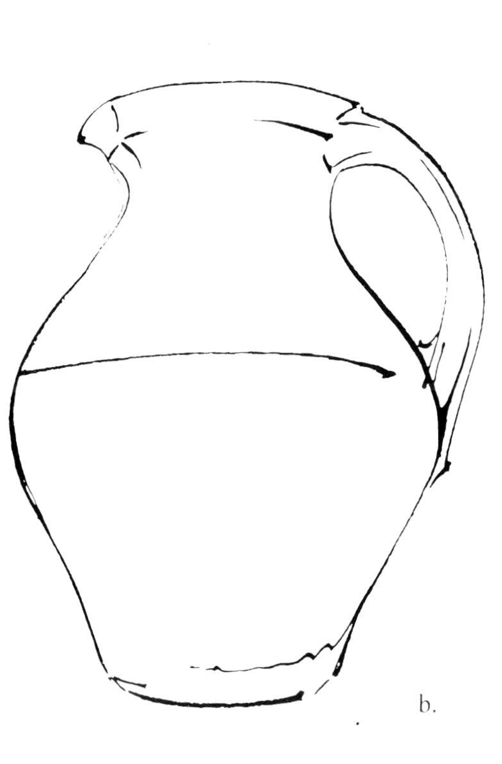
b.

3. The fattest part of the belly is halfway between the base and the narrowest part of the neck and therefore slightly less than halfway up the whole jug. This is *not* a hard and fast rule. I point it out merely to illustrate the interdependency of one element upon another. If the widest part had been lower placed, then

the jug may have appeared rather bottom heavy.

4. The line of growth from the base is often a slightly inward or concave curve (see Jim Malone's bottle on page 63). This together with the angle of growth imparts a sense of lift. The length of this line also has an effect: it is the main line of growth to the belly and handled correctly can be effective in reducing the visual weight of a pot.

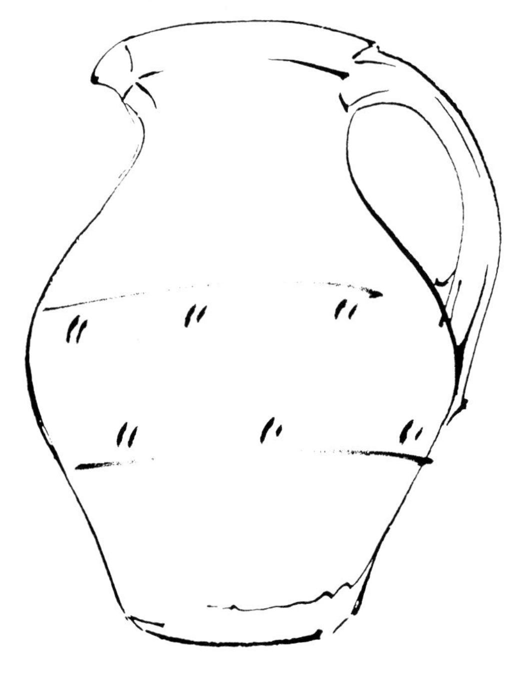

5. Is there going to be any decoration and if so where will it be placed? Decorating any round shape is very difficult indeed. It is often a good idea to break up the rounded surface into smaller areas or panels that are easier to contend with. In the drawing above, I have drawn a line in the clay to coincide with the lower joint of the handle and another just above it. I now have a strip or panel to decorate that seems to fall into place with the handle termination.

All of these points are examples of the kind of questions that you should be asking yourself as you make a pot. Not just jugs but all pots. At first, the answers will be hard to find. Often a shape will appear 'right' to your eyes and 'wrong' to the more experienced eye. That state of affairs will change as your experience and knowledge increase. As a beginner the only advice that I can give you is to be aware of these problems. Do not settle for a shape if you can see right away that it is wrong and to look, look, look at as many pots as you can find.

The sketchbook

However good or bad your drawing, a sketchbook should be an essential part of any potter's equipment. I fill pages and pages of quick, thumbnail sketches of ideas for shapes and variations on themes, many of which will never be used. Your sketchbook can act as a filter for your ideas, weeding out those which are not so good and spotlighting those which have potential. Often by making a drawing of a pot, I am re-affirming that shape in my mind before I sit down to make it. I can remove some of the confusion of form that sometimes occurs in the mind's eye by making a visual representation on paper. ***Remember*** though, that your drawing may not transfer from paper to clay satisfactorily. It is sometimes the case that a 2-D representation does not always work in 3-D so you will have to re-access your idea when you have your pot in front of you.

My sketchbooks form a library of material that I can refer to even years later. Ideas come and go, one moves on from one area of interest to another but an idea that may seem not worth

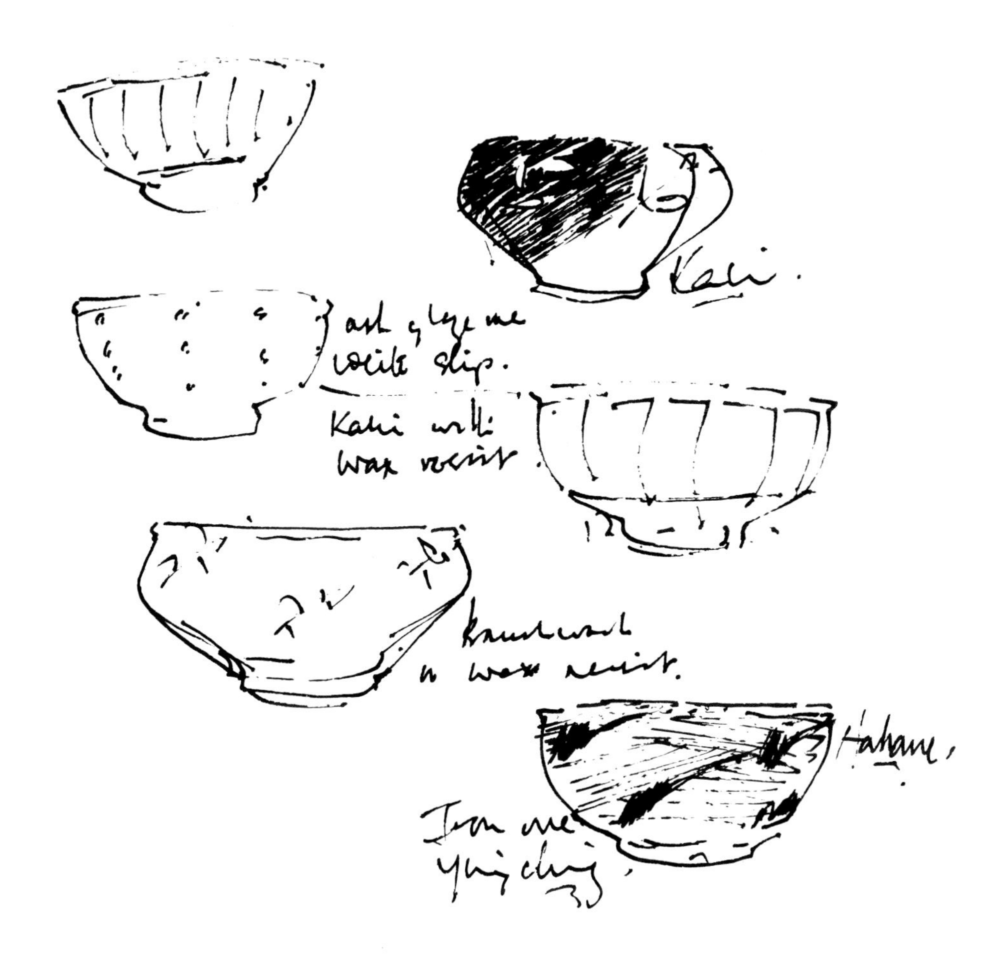

pursuing today may be just what you want tomorrow so don't throw anything away.

You can also use your sketchbook to record pots that you have seen or material that could provide decoration for your pots. A branch with leaves or a flower on a plant, perhaps an interesting fossil or rock formation, nothing commits a shape to the memory better than drawing it however good or bad your drawing may be.

Personal style

This book is primarily for those who are new to making pots on a potter's wheel or those who have mastered the basics and are beginning to feel their way forward. The development of a distinctive personal style is probably a long way in the future although, it is true that everyone, even the beginner, has a 'personal style' to a degree in that no two persons approach clay in the same way. It is the individual's inherent and quite personal 'feel' in the handling of clay and his or her response to other pots that will eventually mark his pots out from someone else's.

The development of a personal vocabulary or style in pottery making is very difficult indeed and many never achieve it even after a life-long career in pottery. Some would argue that it isn't even necessary; that to make good, honest pots that function while enriching the life of the user is enough. To a certain extent I would agree with that sentiment. I would certainly rather see a good pot made in a traditional style than something that struggles to be different or innovative purely for the sake of it. However, I also feel that it is partly our job as potters to take the craft further along its long road of development, otherwise stagnation sets in.

So, what is a personal style? We all know it when we see it; it allows us to tell one potter's work from another. But it's more than that. A potter who makes fine porcelain is easy to tell apart from a potter who makes rugged stoneware. What then about the difference between two stoneware potters? or even harder, two stoneware potters who have chosen to work with similar source references?

Personal style can be reflected in the decoration. Brushwork is often like handwriting and immediately introduces a personal element. Style can be the way that a handle is terminated or the shape of a spout. It can be a glaze or a characteristic form. It can be a vigorous approach to throwing or the shape of a lid. It can be any number of characteristics but most often it is a combination of all these things and more. What is important is that there exists a continuity throughout a potter's repertoire, a kind of working fingerprint that you come to feel comfortable with.

Chapter Thirteen
A Step Further On

As you look at more and more pottery in museums or craft galleries you will see pots that excite and inspire you. Some of these pieces will have been made with techniques that are quite complicated, the mechanics of which will not be immediately apparent to an inexperienced viewer. As your throwing skills increase, you will begin to work out how some of these things were done and begin to feel confident enough to have a go yourself.

I learnt many of the rudimentary skills in this way. Not having had the benefit of a pottery training I would go to a particular craft gallery in Cambridge and spend time looking and inspecting pots, trying to work out in my mind how the different parts had been made. I then went home and, without trying to 'copy' the entire pot, I would try to master a particular element e.g. the seating for a particular lid or the lid itself. In this way and with many, many mistakes I began to build up a potting 'vocabulary' of techniques.

Join a regional potters group. All over the UK, Australia and the USA there are local potters associations that welcome even the newest of beginners. You will find that the association will organise lectures and demonstrations by well-known potters, maybe even hands on workshops where you can learn and exchange techniques not only about throwing but all aspects of pottery. Later, as you progress there will be exhibitions that you can enter that will give you the opportunity to show and perhaps sell your work. At the very least, you may receive qualified and constructive criticism. Your regional potters group is well worth joining. I know that in my case the South Wales Potters gave me my earliest opportunities to learn and to exhibit and I shall always be grateful to them.

Remember, in pottery there are very few hard and fast rules and most of those that do exist are concerned with keeping your pot in one piece once it is finished rather than what you make or how you make it. If you have an idea about a new shape then have a go, nobody is standing behind you ready to reprimand you if you fail. I would say though, that too many failures can make you feel frustrated and angry with yourself or the clay. Always be trying to extend yourself beyond that which you feel comfortable, that's how we all progress, but take small steps rather than big leaps.

In this section I have put together some photographs of pots that were made with unusual techniques. All were thrown but most of them have been altered in one way or another to take the pot away from the perfect symmetry of the potter's wheel. Asymmetry can, in the right hands, impart movement and interest to a pot but it has to be handled in a controlled and masterly fashion otherwise the result can be just a contrived mess.

Left
A large anagama fired jar by Nic Collins (UK), 25 in/63.5 cm tall.
This monumental pot was thrown in two stages. Initially a 15lb ball of clay was thrown to the shape of the lower half of the pot. Later, after allowing the first stage to dry and therefore become firm enough to support the upper half, a second ball of clay was thrown into a thick, round collar. The heavy collar was then turned over still attached to the bat on which it was thrown and joined to the rim of the lower half. Finally, the thick collar was thrown upward and shaped to fit and compliment the lower half.

Nic Collins works in Devon, England and fires in an anagama kiln over a number of days searching for the decorative effects of the fire and ash to grace his pots.

East, which starts from a thrown base which is as high as you wish to make it. After this has firmed up a little, a thick coil is added to the rim and this is then thrown upward. After being allowed to firm up again, another coil is added and the process repeated until the desired height and shape is achieved. The rim should be scored and slip added before each coil is joined. Some potters artificially dry the rim with hot air or a blow lamp prior to the adding of each coil so that quicker progress can be made.

Jeff Mincham lives and works in Australia. His raku pots are often large-scale and ceremonial in nature. His work is represented in many collections both in Australia and around the world.

A faceted ginger jar by Ruthanne Tudball (UK), 10 in/22.5 cm tall.
Ruthanne Tudball has developed a personal style in her throwing that produces pots with great movement and energy. As much as possible the pots are finished when they come off the wheel e.g. teapots are thrown and assembled all in one continuous making process and come from the wheel with their spouts and handles in place. There is no allowance made for the very soft clay, that very softness being used for its decorative quality.

In this large faceted ginger jar the facets have been cut with a twisted wire while the pot was slowly revolving. This diagonal direction to the cut coupled with the lines from the wire and the texture-seeking soda glaze has created a pot with grace and energy.

You can try this technique by using the same cutting tool that I used to make the small faceted teabowl or *Yunomi*. It is a cheese cutter and available from kitchen shops. If you buy the type that allows you to change or replace the wire, then a twisted wire can be inserted instead of the smooth one that is supplied with the tool. Start your cut from the base and work upwards and across in one confident, flowing movement. Don't forget to leave the wall of the pot thicker than normal to allow for the cut to take place. You can shape the jar from the inside after the cuts have been made. This is a difficult technique so don't be put off if at first you don't succeed!

An oval dish with added feet by Joseph Bennion (USA).

To many this dish may seem minimalist. There is indeed a simplicity of form and freedom in the throwing that seems wholly appropriate to the salt-glazed surface. Notice though, the playful management of scale in the size of the handles. The feet are modelled additions and serve to lift the pot physically and visually. This dish is proof that a pot need not be complicated or have unnecessary embellishment to make it a successful piece of work. It is though, important to understand the sophisticated and subtle considerations that have taken place to arrive at such a satisfying solution.

Joseph Bennion works in Spring City, Utah, USA

There are two methods of making a wide, flat circular dish into an oval shape.

1. Throw a wide, shallow dish with the walls as high as you want them but without a base. In effect a 'ring'.

2. Allow this ring to firm up a little, wire it off from the bat and gently manipulate it into an oval shape.

3. Throw a flat disc of clay the thickness of which should be similar to the thickness of the wall of your ring at its base.

4. Place the ring onto the base and join securely together by scoring and slipping the joint.

5. Clean off the excess clay later when base and pot are firm enough to be turned over onto the rim.

The second method is the old 'country' potters' method.

1. Throw a flat bottomed, wide dish.
2. When the dish is firmer but still quite soft, cut a leaf shape from the base.
3. Push the walls of the dish together so that the leaf closes together.
4. Refill the partial opening that is left with the clay that you originally took away and clean up the joint inside and out.

Two 'squared' dishes by Josie Walter (UK). These two dishes are what we call 'slipware', that is to say the decoration is carried out in coloured slips either painted onto the pot's damp surface or trailed on by means of a 'slip trailer', the potter's version of the baker's icing bag. Slipware is a particularly European tradition that has its beginnings in medieval pottery but was at its most spectacular best in the 18th century.

Josie Walter continues in the slipware tradition bringing it up to date with lively and colourful images from everyday life.

Again there are two methods of producing a 'square' dish. You could use the same 'two part' method as I have outlined for the oval dish. A second, slightly more complicated, but much less prone to cracking method is as follows:

1. Throw a normal, circular dish.
2. Take a wire and make a horizontal cut into the wall of the dish at a point equivalent to the level of the floor of the base inside the dish. Bring the wire into the pot about $1\frac{1}{2}$ in/4 cm at the widest point and then carefully take the wire back out again exactly following the line of the cut you have already made.
3. Repeat the process exactly opposite to your first cut.
4. With clean hands carefully lift the wall, move it inwards and rejoin it to the base. Repeat on the other side.
5. After the dish has become firm, turn it over onto its rim on a clean surface (I use a newspaper) and clean away the excess clay with a throwing rib.

Photograph by Lu Jeffery.

Suggested Weights for Specific Pots

The following is a list of suggested weights for items of domestic pottery that most potters will want to make at one time or another. These weights are only a guide. You must weigh your clay *every time* before you start work and keep a record of those weights so that next time you will know exactly how much

Item	Fired Size	Weight lb. oz.	Weight kg g
Mug	3½ in/9 cm 3 in/7.5 cm	12 oz.	340 g
Jug	⅓ pt/0.2 L	12 oz.	340 g
Jug	1 pt/0.6 L	1 lb. 4 oz.	566 g
Teapot (body)	5 in/12.75 cm 5½ in/14.25 cm	2 lb. 4 oz.	1020 g
Teapot (Spout)		8 oz.	226 g
Teapot (lid)	'Sit on' type	8 oz.	226 g
Cereal bowl	5 in/12.75 cm dia. unturned.	1 lb. 2 oz.	510 g
Yunomi	4 in/10 cm 3 in/7.5 cm (turned)	1 lb. 4 oz.	566 g
Teaplate	5 in/12.75 cm dia. (flat)	1 lb. 8 oz.	792 g
Dinner plate	9 in/23 cm dia. (flat)	2 lb. 8 oz.	1358 g
Casserole*	10 in/25 cm dia. 3½ in/ 9 cm	5 lb. 8 oz.	2490 g
Casserole (lid)		6 lb.	2718 g

*Note that the wider a pot becomes, the greater proportionately the weight for the lid. You can see that in this casserole the weight for the lid is actually slightly more than that for the pot. This, of course, is because the lid requires considerable turning. A rounder, less flat pot with a smaller opening would require less clay. This all seems rather obvious but a greater weight for a lid than for the pot is not a concept that is fully appreciated by newcomers to throwing.

Remember: these weights are only a guide. All sizes are approximate as no two potters would make the same sized pot from a given weight of clay.

clay to use. Particularly important is to keep a record of the amount of clay required for the lids for a range of diameters. You will then have an instant reference for, let's say a 4 in. opening for a storejar or an 8 in. opening for a casserole.

If you record the weights that you use, you will soon develop an intuitive feeling for the required weight of clay to give a particular volume or height. Also, by keeping records you will easily know how much to lessen or increase a weight should you feel that the last batch of a particular type of pot was either too small or too large. In the early stages of throwing you will probably find that you will use more clay per pot than you really need to. Another benefit of weighing your clay is that you will be able to measure your improving skills as the weight required to make a particular pot decreases a little.

Places Where You Can See Fine Quality Pottery

I have said in the text of this book that it is essential for any potter, beginner or professional to look at, hold and carefully inspect the very best of pottery that is available to be seen. To this end I am including the following list which is by no means exhaustive but which may help you initially in searching out examples of both historical and contemporary pots that will help you in your own development.

Southern England

Contemporary Ceramics, Marshall Street, London. Tel. 071 437 7605.
(The foremost outlet for the best work from British potters who are all fellows of the Craft Potters Association of Great Britain.)

Contemporary Applied Arts, 43 Earlham Street, London. Tel. 071 836 6993.
(A mix of the very best of British Crafts including pottery and ceramics.)

Victoria and Albert Museum, Cromwell Road, London. Tel. 071 938 8500.
(Vast collection of pottery and ceramics from all over the world covering many centuries plus 20th century British studio ceramics.)

British Museum, Great Russell Street, London Tel. 071 636 1555.
(Medieval and later pots including slipwares. Vast collections of oriental ceramics.)

Ashmolean Museum, Oxford. Tel. 0865 278000.
(Vast, internationally renowned collection of ceramics including Chinese and Korean.)

Crafts Council, 44a Pentonville Road, London N1 9BY. Tel. 071 938 8500.
(Temporary exhibitions that often include pottery, slide index with public access and National Collection of Craft viewed by appointment.)

Oxford Gallery, 23 High Street, Oxford. Tel. 0865 242731.
(Commercial gallery, mixed craft with a high proportion of quality pottery.)

South West England

Tate Gallery, St Ives, Cornwall.
(Wingfield Digby Collection.) Bernard Leach, Hamada, Cardew, Bouverie, Marshall etc.

New Craftsman Gallery, Fore Street, St Ives, Cornwall. Tel. 0736 795652.
(Contemporary ceramics plus a selection of older studio pots.)

Leach Pottery, St Ives, Cornwall.
Tel. 0736 796398.
(Collection of Bernard Leach's pots.)

Holburne Museum and Crafts Study Centre, Great Pulteney Street, Bath.
Tel. 0225 466669.
(Collection including Bernard Leach, Katherine Pleydell Bouverie and others.)

Museum of North Devon, The Square, Barnstaple, Devon. Tel. 0271 46747.
(Devon country pottery including slipwares.)

Portsmouth City Museum, Museum Road, Portsmouth. Tel. 0705 827261.
(Large collection of 20th century ceramics.)

City Art Gallery, Southampton.
Tel. 0703 832277.
(Part of the Milner-White collection available to view by appointment.)

Exeter Museum, Queen Street, Exeter, Devon. Tel. 0392 456724.
(20th century British studio pottery.)

Devon Guild of Craftsmen, Riverside Mill, Bovey Tracey, Devon. Tel. 0626 832223.
(Mixed crafts from Devon but includes a high proportion of good quality pottery.)

East of England

Fitzwilliam Museum, Trumpington Street, Cambridge. Tel. 0223 332900.
(Small collection of 20th century work but also historical examples particularly medieval English.)

Midlands

City Museum and Art Gallery, Bethesda Street, Stoke on Trent. Tel. 0782 202173.
(Houses the Henry Bergen collection of early British studio pottery plus examples of later work. Also Staffordshire slipware, early salt glaze and much more.)

City Art Gallery, Moseley Street, Manchester. Tel. 061 236 5244.
(Small but representative collection of 20th century studio pots plus historical examples.)

Liverpool Museum, William Brown Street, Liverpool. Tel. 051 207 0001.
(Large collection of British studio pottery including the finest pot by Hamada I have seen in this country. Also vast collection of Liverpool Delft.)

Bluecoat Centre, School Lane, Liverpool.
Tel. 051 709 4014.
(Mixed craft gallery but includes a high proportion of pottery.)

Derby University, Derby. 0332 347181.
(Rollo Ballantyne collection of 20th century studio ceramics.)

Leicestershire Museum, 96 New Walk, Leicester. Tel. 0533 554100.
(Good spread of 20th century studio potters.)

North of England

City Art Gallery, York. Tel. 0904 623839.
(Milner White collection including Leach, Hamada, Cardew etc.)

Cleveland Crafts Centre, 57 Gilkes Street, Middlesbrough. Tel. 0642 226351.
(Extensive collection of 20th century British potters.)

Shipley Art Gallery, Prince Consort Road, Gateshead. Tel. 091 477 1495.
(Permanent collection of studio ceramics and intermittant temporary exhibitions.)

Scotland

Paisley Museum, High Street, Paisley.
Tel. 041 889 3151.
(Huge collection of British studio ceramics.)

The Open Eye Gallery, Cumberland Street, Edinburgh. Tel. 031 557 1020.
(Commercial gallery. Pottery in

permanent stock plus temporary exhibition programme.)

Wales

Aberystwyth Arts Centre, Penglais Hill, Aberystwyth. Tel. 0970 622882.
(University of Wales collection of ceramics including studio pots particularly Michael Cardew, Welsh slipwares, Martin Brothers, Oriental etc. Also programme of temporary exhibitions by leading potters.)

National Museum of Wales, Cardiff. Tel. 0222 397951.
(Some 20th century works including Bernard Leach. Historical examples including slipwares.)

Welsh Folk Museum, Saint Fagans, Cardiff. Tel. 0222 569441.
(Country pottery from medieval to 20th century including Welsh slipwares from Buckley and Ewenny.)

'Spectrum', Maengwyn Street, Machynleth, Powys. Tel. 0654 702877.
(Commercial gallery with large stock of excellent studio pots.)

Porticus, Middleton Street, Llandrindod Wells. Tel. 0597 823989.
(Commercial gallery with a good selection of pottery.)

Newport Museum and Art Gallery, John Frost Square, Newport, Gwent. Tel. 0633 840064.

(Collection of studio pottery and in particular teapots.)

Northern Ireland

Ulster Museum, Botanic Gardens, Belfast. Tel. 0232 381251.
(Large and comprehensive collection of 20th century studio pottery.)

There are many, many more museums and art galleries that have collections of pottery both historical and contemporary. Check out your local museum and see what they have to offer. The Crafts Council 'Crafts Map' is a guide to all craft shops and galleries that have been listed for quality by the Crafts Council and is available from them at the above number. The Craft Potters Association of Great Britain publishes *Potters* which is a directory of all the members of the association. The book illustrates each potter's work and gives the addresses and telephone numbers of over 200 British potters. *Potters* is available from *Ceramic Review* Books, 21 Carnaby Street, London or at Contemporary Ceramics at the address above.

Suggested Further Reading

There are many books on pottery available. Some are good and some, I'm afraid, not so good. Generally speaking those books that are written by top quality, practising potters tend to be excellent. If you want to buy further books that you feel will help you, my advice is to check out the author's credentials. There are books available which are supposed to be teaching books that are full of glossy photographs and not a lot else! That may be because the author hasn't got a lot to say. Not all the books in this list are 'how to do it' books. Some show photographs of exemplary pots, others contain photographs but also contain insights into the life and thoughts of the potter.

The following is a short reading list that I can recommend and that I feel sure will be a great help.

Books

Birks, Tony and Cornelia Wingfield Digby, *Bernard Leach, Hamada and their Circle*, Phaidon.

Casson, Michael, *The Craft of the Potter*, BBC Books.

Ceramic Review Book of Clays and Glazes, Craft Potters Association of Great Britain.

Gibson, John, *Pottery Decoration*, A & C Black.

Hamer, Frank & Janet, *The Potter's Dictionary of Materials and Techniques*, A & C Black.

Leach, Bernard, *Hamada – Potter*, Kodansha.

Leach, Bernard, *A Potter's Book*, Faber and Faber.

Peterson, Susan, *Shoji Hamada*, Kodansha.

Phethean, Richard, *Throwing*, Batsford.

POTTERS, Directory of British Potters who are members of the Craft Potters Association of Great Britain.

Rackham, Bernard, *Medieval English Pottery*, Faber and Faber. (Sadly out of print but can still be found in good secondhand bookshops.)

Riddick, Sarah, *Pioneer Studio Pottery*, Lund Humphries.

Magazines

Ceramic Review is bi-monthly and available from 21 Carnaby Street, London WIV 1PH.

Ceramics Monthly is available from 1609 Northwest Boulevard, Box 12448, Columbus, Ohio 43212. USA.

Ceramics Art and Perception is quarterly and available from 35 William Street, Paddington, NSW 2021, Australia.

Studio Pottery is bi-monthly and available from *Studio Pottery*, 15 Magdalen Road, Exeter, Devon EX2 4TA.

Pottery Suppliers

The following is a list of some of the potters supplies companies. I suggest that you write off to some of them and ask for their catalogues and price lists. Many of them will supply small clay samples at little or no cost. Try them out and find a clay body that suits your needs and taste. Remember that, generally, the more you buy the cheaper it becomes.

North American Suppliers

American Art Clay Company 4717 W. 16th Street, Indianapolis IN 46222 (tel. 317 244 6871)

Axner Pottery Supply
PO Box 621484, Oviedo FL 32765 (tel. 800 843 7057)

Continental Clay Company
1101 Stinson Blvd, N.E., Minneapolis MN 55413 (tel. 612 331 9332)

Laguna Clay Company
14400 Lomitas Avenue, City of Industry CA 91746 (tel. 800 452 4862)

Mile Hi Ceramics
77 Lipan, Denver, Colorado 80205 (tel. 800 456 0163)

Minnesota Clay Co.
8001 Grand Avenue South, Bloomington MN 55420 (tel. 612884 9101)

Tucker's Pottery Supplies Inc.
15 West Pearce Street, Unit 7, Richmond Hill, Ontario L4B 1H6 (tel. 800 304 6185)

The Potters Shop
31 Thorpe Road, Needham Heights, MA 02194 (tel. 781 449 7687)

UK Suppliers

Bath Potters Supplies
2 Dorset Close, Bath BA2 3RF (tel. 01225 337046)

Briar Wheels & Supplies, Whitsbury Road, Fordingbridge, Hampshire SP6 1NQ (tel. 01425 652991)

Brick House Ceramic Supplies
The Barns, Sheepcote Farm, Sheepcote Lane, Silverend, Witham, Essex CM8 3PJ (tel. 01376 585655)

Clayman
251b Pagham Road, Nyetimber, Bognor Regis, West Sussex, PO21 3QB (tel. 01243 265845)

K.F.S. Acme Marls Ltd.
Bournes Bank, Burslem, Stoke-on-Trent, Staffs. ST6 3DW (tel. 01782 577757)

Potclays Ltd.
Brickkiln Lane, Etruria, Stoke-on-Trent ST1 5SS (tel. 01782 219816)

Potterycrafts Ltd.
Cambell Road, Stoke-on-Trent, ST4 4ET (tel. 01782 745000)

WJ Doble Pottery Clays
Newdowns Sand & Clay Pits, St. Agnes, Cornwall, TR5 0ST (tel. 01872 552979)

Right
A square, salt-glazed bottle by the Author, h. 15 in. The decoration on this bottle was drawn through a wet coating of slip with a chisel-ended wooden tool with a serrated edge.

Index